All About Trout

All About Trout

Complete Angler's Library ®
North American Fishing Club
Minneapolis, Minnesota

All About Trout

TH

Copyright © 1991, North American Fishing Club

All rights reserved.

Library of Congress Catalog Card Number 91-60836
ISBN 0-914697-38-2

Printed in U.S.A.
        12   13   14   15   16   17   18

Contents

Tackle For Trout

Streams

Lakes And Reservoirs

Acknowledgments

The North American Fishing Club would like to thank everyone who helped with the creation of this book.

Wildlife artist Virgil Beck created the cover art; artists David Rottinghaus and John A. (Buzz) Buczynski created all illustrations. The author, John Holt, provided many of the photographs throughout the book. Outdoor photographers C. Boyd Pfeiffer and Dale Spartas contributed additional photos along with North American Fishing Club's Managing Editor Steve Pennaz and Managing Editor of Books Ron Larsen.

A special thanks to the Fishing Club's publication staff for their efforts: Editor and Publisher Mark LaBarbera, Managing Editor Steve Pennaz, Managing Editor of Books Ron Larsen, Editorial Assistant Colleen Ferguson and Layout Artist Dean Peters. Thanks also to Vice President of Product Marketing Mike Vail, Marketing Manager Cal Franklin and Marketing Project Coordinator Laura Resnik.

About The Author

John Holt enjoys fishing for every kind of fish imaginable, using different methods and equipment. However, he especially loves fishing for trout. He says trout can be one of the most exciting and rewarding fish to catch. Aside from his personal involvement with the sport of fishing, John is a free-lance writer specializing in conservation, travel and outdoors. His informative and entertaining articles have appeared in a variety of publications including *Fly Fisherman, Fly Rod & Reel, Fly Fishing, The Denver Post, Gray's Sporting Journal, Field & Stream, The Angling Report, Chevy Outdoors and Travel & Leisure.* He has also written a book, *Knee-Deep In Montana's Trout Streams,* which is expected to be released by Pruett Publishing, and is working on its sequel.

John, who was born in Washington D.C. and raised in the Midwest, has been catching fish since he was about five years old. His angling experiences have taken him to a number of breath-taking and unusual places in Ireland, France, Morocco, Canada and throughout the United States. One of his most memorable and fascinating fishing experiences was fishing in Morocco with Africans. He said he was happy to have had that opportunity to see how they live. Given today's political atmosphere there, even if he wanted to, he could not repeat his adventure today.

John's love for writing grew after attending the University of Montana where he majored in creative writing and double-minored in astronomy and history. He then began his career by combining his writing skills with his outdoors experience and expertise.

In addition to his favorite sport of fishing for trout, John's hobbies include photography and hiking. John's love for the outdoors shines through with his choice of living arrangements. He lives in what he believes to be one of the most scenic and beautiful places in the world—Whitefish, Montana. A number of nature's greatest wilderness creations are in his part of the world (where he fishes extensively). To the east of Whitefish is the Glacier National Park and to the south is Flathead Lake. When John looks out his window, he can see the towering, majestic Rocky Mountains.

John says he has had many adventures in his lifetime and plans to continue having them. He is happily married to his wife Lynda and has three children. Their names are Jack, Elizabeth and Rachel.

Dedication

For Jack, Elizabeth and Rachel

Foreword

Fishing for carp on the Mississippi River was my passion as I grew up, but I've had enough fun-filled experiences fishing for trout to know that there are some anglers who want to make the sport more complicated than it really has to be. Sure, one of the greatest thrills in fishing is watching a trophy brown take a dry fly drifting over his feeding lie. But it's also a tremendous thrill to take that same brown on ultra-light spinning gear and a small spinner or plug. And who's to say the one fish a child will remember for the rest of his or her life couldn't be a trout taken behind a downrigger ball?

The purpose of this book is not to convert you to a certain style or type of fishing, it's to help you catch more trout. That means we will be looking way beyond just flies and fly fishing. We'll look at the fish themselves, concentrating on their needs, habits and preferences in ways that will help you interpret conditions you encounter while fishing. Then, we begin a concise course in finding trout. We'll cover all types of waters including rivers and streams, spring creeks, lakes and reservoirs, and the mighty Great Lakes. Trout thrive in a variety of lakes and streams, and fantastic fishing awaits those who know how to unlock their secrets.

This book, while not meant to be a scientific study of the various species, does go into detail about the private lives of the most popular species of trout—browns, rainbows, brookies, cutthroats, bulls, goldens and lakers—as well as some of their relatives like grayling and char. We'll talk about their ranges, distinctive features, favorite foods and likely holding areas—little-known information that will help you immensely every time you're on the water.

We'll also show how to properly outfit yourself for successful trout fishing. We approach the subject in a way that is easy to understand, even for beginning anglers, but we go way beyond the basics. We'll discuss fly, spinning and baitcasting tackle, each one's strengths and weaknesses, and how to use them properly.

Fly fishing can be an intimidating topic for many anglers because of all the variables involved so we dedicated an entire chapter to trout fishing hardware and fly lines, including how to select the right ones for the type of fishing you do most.

We've also included chapters on trout lures, including spinners, spoons and plugs, and live bait for those times when nothing else seems to work as well. There is even a chapter on miscellaneous gear that will help make your trout fishing more fun and productive.

We'll also share dozens of little-known tips that can spell the difference between success and failure. We'll look at trout's natural wariness and suggest important ways to minimize its negative effects on your catch rates. We're not just talking about ways to improve your presentations, either. Though important, natural presentations are only a small part of the overall fish-catching process. Equipment selection, wading skills and other aspects are equally important. It's impossible to catch a fish that has been spooked by a careless approach.

As another example of this book's completeness, in a section covering all types of streams, we take an in-depth look at the different types of trout waters that fall within the category of streams and tell you how to identify the prime fish-holding areas. For all types of moving water, we'll tell you what prime lies are and how to find them. We'll also show you how to properly fish riffles and runs, pools, undercut banks and more. This information will not only help you catch more trout, it will help you catch salmon, bass, walleyes and other fish that thrive in moving waters.

The book's final section does the same thing for those of you who pursue trout in lakes and reservoirs. We'll cover downrigging and other techniques used by anglers in boats, as well as things bank-bound anglers can do to improve their success. This section will also outline general seasonal patterns to help you find trout no matter what time of year you fish.

By now, I hope it's obvious that this book is much different from any others you've probably read on trout fishing. We've thrown biases aside and looked at fishing trout through eyes not clouded by tradition. If you do the same thing, you'll catch more fish—I guarantee it!

Steve Pennaz,
Executive Director
North American Fishing Club

Understanding Trout

1

The History And Romance Of Trout Fishing

Throughout history, no other family of fish has engendered more outpouring of passion, myth, scholarship and even snobbery than the trout. Indeed, trout fishing has such a long and ancient lineage that just tracing the pursuit has become a specialized area of study for scholars of the arcane. Books have been written on this subject alone.

As for the trout themselves, including the romance, history, skills and techniques needed to catch them, more has been written on these fish than on all other species combined, despite the fact that most anglers fish for bass or panfish in this country. There is something mysterious about trout—something which cannot be quantified that exerts a powerful hold on dedicated anglers.

With few exceptions, the places NAFC members find trout are also places of beauty and relatively unspoiled character. From the classic limestone creeks and rivers of the Northeast to the small mountain brooks of the Smoky Mountains, to the free-flowing brawling rivers of the West and on up to the high-mountain lakes of the Rockies, the search for trout takes a person to some pretty fine country.

Taking nothing away from the noble carp, but where would you rather fish? In some turbid, polluted river sliding greasily through an industrial city or on a sparkling clear trout stream with the smell of pine drifting on a cool breeze with

A healthy stream brown trout taken on a fly rod puts life into the romance and aura of trout fishing. It makes your heart beat faster, providing a feeling of exhilaration.

The History And Romance Of Trout Fishing

Tying The Snell Knot

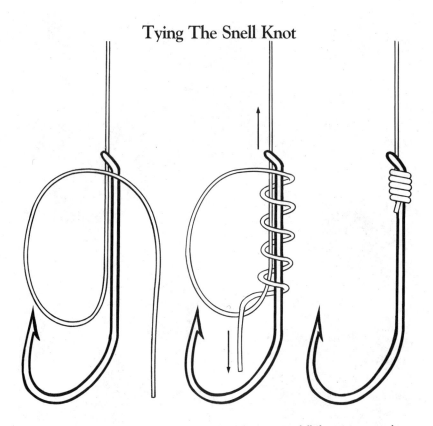

Part of the romance of trout fishing is that trout fishermen are skilled at tying exotic knots. While its use is not limited to trout fishing, the snell knot is one closely associated with the sport. This diagram shows how it is tied.

snowcapped mountains defining the horizon. For most of us, the choice is not a difficult one.

When you factor in the beauty of the trout themselves, the hook that holds us is a well-conceived one. From the strong yellow flanks dotted with crimson spots of the brown, to the silvery sleakness of a rainbow, to the cartoon-like pinks, oranges and yellows of a golden trout, every species has an unchecked beauty that bursts into magnificence as they thrash the surface at the ends of our lines. All wild trout are beautiful fish—wonders to behold and to hold in our hands. They are perfect reflections of their unspoiled habitats.

But there is much more to the magic associated with trout. There are times when the fish are so easy to catch that a person actually begins to believe that he knows everything there is to know about these fish, that he can pull up to a river, lake or pond whenever he desires and take trout on every cast.

Then, there are those maddening outings where you fling every spoon, spinner, plug, fly, worm, hellgramite and grasshopper in your possession at the fish and nothing comes of the efforts. And to make matters worse, the fish, usually large colorful ones, can be seen feeding along the bottom or rising with delicate style right next to where you last cast.

Finding The Fish Is Only Half The Battle

Finding fish is the first prerequisite for catching fish, but knowing just exactly where trout are holding is often only the beginning of a challenging (and perhaps frustrating) day on the open water.

Working the line between shallow water and drop-offs is an effective fish-finding tactic that often results in plenty of big fish throughout the day, but it can be particularly effective during the evening.

Anglers have documented the various difficulties of catching trout for centuries. Izaak Walton published the *Compleat Angler* in 1653 (and there were plenty of books on the subject of trout fishing even before then).

"And before you begin to angle, cast to have the wind on your back, and the sun, if it shines, to be before you, and to fish down the stream; and carry the point or top of your rod downward, by which means the shadow of yourself, and rod too, will be the least offensive to the fish; for the sight of any shade amazes the fish, and spoils your sport, of which you must take great care."

One simple paragraph contained a wealth of knowledge and experience ranging from technique to approach to trout behavior. There is no doubt Walton knew his subject judging from the fact that his book has appeared in well over 400 different editions.

We have been fishing for trout since the first arrivals more than half of a millennium ago. The native tribes, who roamed North America for many thousands of years prior to the pilgrims' landings, relied quite heavily on trout as an important food source.

Documentation indicates that sportsmen have fished for trout since the 18th century in this country. Later, they became so concerned with the possible loss of their recreational trout fishery that they went so far as to import brown trout from their native European waters to replace diminishing populations of brook trout as early as in the 1880s.

A number of organizations, including Trout Unlimited and the Federation of Flyfishers, devote many hours to preserving and enhancing our trout waters.

Flying ahead through time nearly 300 years from Walton's day to 1938, we find a brief consideration of Ray Bergman's dedication to the classic volume *Trout* lends further insight into the fascination and wonder these fish hold over us:

"To you all, the many good fellows I know and have fished with, and those whose paths may never cross mine except through the medium of these pages. This is my visit with you, our fishing adventures together. I trust it will be enjoyable, instructive, and memorable. When I am gone, when all who now read these pages have passed beyond, I hope Trout will continue to live, perhaps instill in future generations a love and understanding of angling."

Reading this, one almost gets the feeling that something far more important is being discussed here than "mere" fishing, and that, too, is part of the romance of the trout. To seek the fish in its native, unspoiled waters is to experience nature as it was before "civilization" reduced much of our wilderness environment to tamed, developed countryside.

To spend any period of time in pristine country far away from cities, highways and cars is to reaffirm our connection with a feral past, to re-establish ties with the cabalistic, primitive, natural lifestyle of our distant ancestors, and that is as much a part of the attraction of trout fishing as anything—a fundamental and important return to the basics, casting off the artificial trappings of "modern" society.

Trout Provide The Means For Escape

For many of us, just getting away from our jobs and out onto the water is as important as actually catching trout.

For many more of us, though, feeling a rainbow-gone-berserk or a hard-charging brown or head-shaking brook trout at the end of our line is a heady brew we can never get enough of no matter how hard we try.

In no other fishing can just one good fish turn a long, hard, disappointing outing into a memory of a lifetime. One big, aggressive trout that stretches both angler and tackle to their limits as it races away in a river or across a lake, instantly transforms hours of tedium and boredom into the stuff of vision quest and hyperbole. Only trout seem to be able to do that for millions of anglers.

With the introduction of so many new materials into the sport of fishing, most anglers can afford decent equipment, although most of us wind up spending small fortunes on our gear. Accumulating rods, reels, lures, flies, hooks, vests, waders, landing nets, knives, creels, lines, hooks, polarized sunglasses, clippers, sinkers—you name it—is a legitimate way to indulge a child's fascination with toys on an "adult" level. Trout fishers are the "bag ladies" of angling. This is another part of the romance and attraction of trout fishing.

Not only do you have spinning and baitcasting gear to

The romance of trout fishing has many facets, but the prime reward is the trout themselves. The angler that caught this 16-inch rainbow beauty will attest to that.

choose from, but there is also an array of fly fishing equipment that staggers the imagination. There are literally dozens of magazines devoted to trout fishing in general and fly fishing in particular. For those who live to read, they need only fill out subscription forms and then await the deluge of printed material, including a staggering selection of catalogs, in order to experience trout fishing vicariously. This is still another aspect of the romance we have with the trout.

Many anglers have a couple of hundred books on trout fishing lining their shelves. A few others have collections of a thousand or more, some of them first editions a couple of hundred years old and more valuable than all of the fishing equipment they have stored away in the dark recesses of their attics, basements and garages.

There are so many facets to catching trout, so many little nooks and corners to capture the imagination, that even if all the trout waters in the world were destroyed by pollution and development, the sport would live on for decades, if not centuries, before exhausting its momentum.

This fact more than any other is the most telling when one tries to explain the attraction of trout to anglers.

More than any other species, trout are creatures of your imaginations and dreams, and the real magic in all of this lies in the fact that these fantasies can be converted to real-life experiences by simply traveling to your favorite lake or stream—by simply rigging up and fishing for the trout.

What more is needed?

2

Brown Trout

Y ou could spend a lifetime trying to catch all of the species and subspecies of the family Salmonidae of which trout (genus Salmo) are members. In reality, brook and lake trout are chars (genus Salvelinus), and recently fisheries biologists have re-classified several Salmos as Oncorhynchus in an attempt to explain (through name change) behavior and appearance characteristics similar to those exhibited by Pacific salmon.

Differences between trout and chars for the angler are minor, chief among them being the fact that trout have dark spots on light backgrounds and chars have light spots on dark backgrounds. Chars also prefer slightly colder water than trout which thrive in temperatures from 50 to 65 degrees with readings over 80 degrees approaching a lethal level. For our purposes, chars will be considered trout, and the Oncorhynchus debate will be left to the scientific community.

For the NAFC member, the major species are brown, rainbow, brook, cutthroat, lake and golden. Brown, rainbow, brook and cutthroat trout have anadromous (fish that migrate from the sea into freshwater to spawn) strains, the most-fished-for being the rainbow's steelhead and the brown's sea trout. These fish will be discussed at length in the chapter on browns and rainbows. A number of other species provide good sport in specific areas of North America such as bull, Dolly Varden, grayling, gila and Apache trout. They will be discussed in the final chapter of this section.

Finally, every trout known to man has been raised with widely varying degrees of success in hatcheries, both private and government operated. A large proportion of today's sport trout fishery is a result of these efforts. But there is little or no comparison between the instincts, native intelligence, sporting qualities and coloring of a hatchery trout and a wild one. Those few raised fish that manage to survive their own ignorance during the first year in the wild gradually take on the attributes of their natural relative. For example, a rainbow fresh from a hatchery will look and fight something like a wild rainbow, but the characteristics that make the rainbow a great gamefish are, at best, muted in the hatchery specimen.

The Crafty Brown Trout

When you want to go hunting for big, crafty, stealthy trout, head for your favorite brown trout water. This species (Salmo trutta) epitomizes predatory sophistication and is a result of thousands of years of evolution. When you land a brown over 5 pounds, you've got a right to be happy and proud. You've earned these basic pleasures.

Brown trout were first widely introduced into North America in 1883 when eggs were shipped to a hatchery in Long Island, New York, by Baron Lucius von Behr. These were to provide a substitute for brook trout, which were disappearing with the encroachment of civilization on their wild, pristine habitat. Browns are native to Europe from the Mediterranean region up to Norway and Siberia including the British Isles. In fact, brown trout are known locally in this country as Loch Leven for their native water in Scotland. The fish have also been introduced into Asia, New Zealand, South America and Africa. Wherever trout fishers wander, they seem to bring along either brood stock or eggs. The brown is one of the most widely distributed trout in the world.

Theodore Gordon, who is considered the "Father of American fly fishing," frequently referred to browns as "yellow trout" because of the predominance of this color along the lower flanks and belly of many specimens, particularly during their fall spawning runs.

The brown trout's body is about five times as long as it is

Brown Trout

Rainbow Trout

Brook Trout

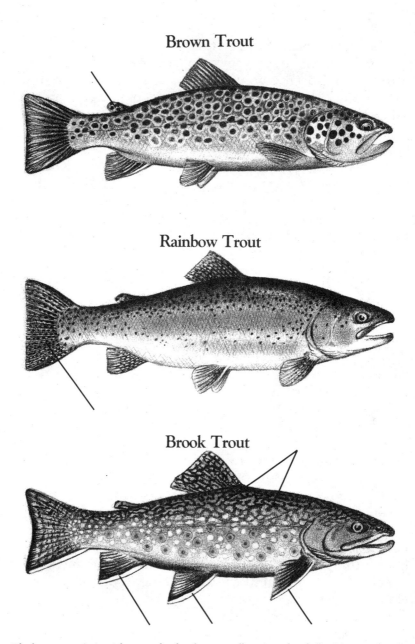

The brown trout's (top) brown sides dissolve into yellow toward its belly. It's spotted with a square tail with few or no spots, and some spots on its adipose fin (line). Its spots often have whitish to bluish halos. Rainbows (center) have radiating rows of black spots over much of the body including the tail, with a pinkish horizontal band and gill cover and no teeth on the tongue. The brook trout (bottom) ranges from brownish to greenish. Its back is laced with light, worm-like marks and the sides have light spots and some red spots, both with blue halos. All lower fins have white leading edges.

Cutthroat Trout

Golden Trout

Lake Trout

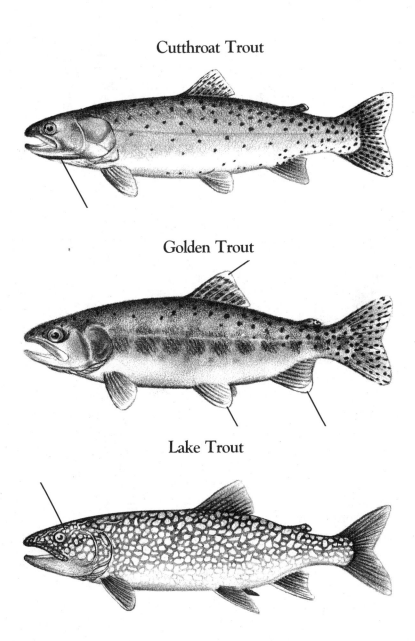

Cutthroat trout (top) have reddish slash marks on the throat, black spots on the tail and a patch of teeth at the base of the tongue. Golden trout (center) have golden sides with a reddish horizontal band which extends along much of the lateral line. About 10 dusky patches, looking like smudges, are spaced along the band. A forked tail is perhaps the easiest identification of a lake trout (bottom) which is really a char. It's heavily spotted with some spots as large as the pupil of the trout's eye.

deep, and its fins (as with all trout) are soft-rayed. They do not have sharp-pointed spines like the dorsal fin of a perch for example. The fish is brown in color, often shading to nearly black on its back. Black spots mark the sides, back and dorsal fin. These are frequently surrounded by a soft halo of silver or much lighter brown. Lesser numbers of crimson or orange spots are often present. The belly may be anywhere from yellow to creamy white. The fins, including the square-shaped tail, are dusky brown.

The tail may also have a number of indistinct spots. The only fish the brown might be confused with is the landlocked salmon of the eastern portion of the continent, but the brown has a double zigzag row of vomerine (middle of the roof of the mouth) teeth while the landlocks are poorly developed.

The Lock Leven version is a still-water strain that is much more silvery than the German fish that contributed the genes responsible for the red and black spots and yellow color of many of today's browns. Because of intrabreeding among the strains, variations in color now are due more to environmental conditions than genetic traits.

Brown trout can reach weights of 40 pounds. Every year anglers regularly take fish of greater than 10 pounds in the western U.S., less often in the East. A 5-pound brown is a big fish in the West. Two pounds generates similar excitement in the East where waters are usually smaller and fishing pressure much more intense. This is all relative, and an angler's scale of perspective seems to adapt almost immediately to an area's conditions. Brown trout usually exceed 18 inches by the sixth year and may live as long as 18 years. They spawn in the fall in moving water that flows over clean gravel where the eggs and milt are deposited. Large females lay several thousand eggs which hatch the following spring. A mature male can always be differentiated from a female because of the male's development of a kype or hooked lower jaw.

Big Browns Like Big Meals

Brown trout feed on aquatic insects such as mayflies, caddis flies and stone flies along with terrestrials and crayfish. Big browns prefer forage fish and other trout including their own kind. Some anglers refer to browns that feed heavily on other

Brown trout, especially big ones, feed extensively on forage fish and smaller trout. A crafty though voracious eater, this hefty brown was taken with a sculpin imitation.

trout as cannibals. They are often caught for the express purpose of removing them from a certain river or lake under the mistaken impression that this will improve the fishing. Usually what happens is that another dominate brown takes up residence in the former's preferred lie and resumes the feeding pattern done in the past.

Browns are often nocturnal feeders, and many of the largest fish are taken after dark, a truly unique experience on a river where maintaining your footing is a sporting proposition in itself as a huge unseen fish tears line off your reel.

There are several subspecies and related species including a race of brown trout in Ireland that feeds entirely on snails. The ohrid trout (Salmo letnica), native to Yugoslavia, was introduced into a few waters in Minnesota, but the fish were found to be slow-growing and late-maturing, decidedly negative character-istics for an introduced sportfish.

Other species that resemble the brown include the softmouth (Salmo obtusirostris) of Yugoslavia which is similar except for a sucker-like mouth; the sevan (Salmo ischchan) of the Soviet Union; and the marble (Salmo mormoratus), also of Yugoslavia, which can exceed 40 pounds and is even more predacious than the brown.

Brown trout have also acquired a reputation of being able to survive in waters where other trout cannot—those waters that are either considered too polluted or too warm. There is some evidence to justify the part concerning tolerance of pollution. For example, large numbers of the trout survive and even thrive in the upper Clark Fork River in western Montana despite heavy concentrations of toxic metals accumulated from decades of mining.

As for temperature, studies seem to indicate that rainbows have a higher upper limit tolerance than browns, despite what many anglers may believe. One of the main reasons for this misconception is that brown trout prefer deep runs and pools, while other species are often found in sparkling mountain streams and fast-flowing riffles—water that gives the appearance of being colder than prime brown-holding areas.

Browns Are Hardest Trout To Catch

Anglers consider brown trout the most difficult to catch, especially when they reach a couple of pounds or more. In Oregon on the Deschutes, one brown was taken for every four rainbow by anglers, and in Maine the ratio was one brown to every five brook trout.

The reason for this is obvious when one examines the locations where big browns are found. The largest fish prefer undercut banks, calm areas in among logjams, deep eddies and pools and powerful runs. This is among the toughest water to fish properly. The trout will not move far to take the lure or bait because the expenditure in energy is too great. So, the angler must get his offering down along the bottom or back under a bank, often among a tangle of roots. The feeding lane for these browns is often no more than a couple of inches wide, a very narrow window of opportunity.

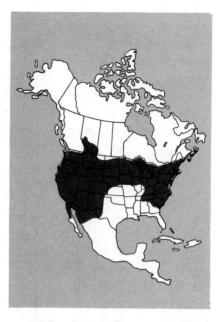

Browns are found throughout the West, North-Central and Northeastern United States, as well as the Canadian Rockies and along the eastern coast of Canada.

What then distinguishes a brown trout from other members of its clan when it comes to feeding and fighting characteristics?

One thing is for sure. If you want to consistently take big browns, you are going to have to use a big bait. You are not going to take very many browns that weigh a couple of pounds or more with a maggot or a $\frac{1}{16}$th-ounce spoon or a No. 24 midge dry. Older browns will not waste their valuable energy chasing the small stuff.

Admittedly, there are times when browns weighing 5 pounds or more gorge themselves on aquatic insects. Summer evenings on the Beaverhead in southwestern Montana will often find large fish cruising the smooth water near shore scooping up mouthfuls of caddis flies that are hatching in such profusion that their mating flights obscure the water's surface and the bankside bushes. Anglers are often unable to catch any of these fish for the simple reason that their flies are lost in the swirling crowd.

At other times on the same river, the damselfly hatch brings the big boys to the surface, but even with the smaller numbers of flying bodies on the water, the angler still has a somewhat difficult time attracting the attention of the browns.

Over the years, fishing down deep for large browns with

Brown Trout

large offerings has proven itself time and time again. Losing tackle is part of the process if you are fishing trophy-fish water properly. Whether this is a large spinner, spoon, minnow or streamer such as a Woolly Bugger, the key is to locate the deepest, nastiest, most-secure looking water a river has to offer.

If there is a tangle of small tree limbs submerged next to a wide curve in a stream with an undercut bank filled with exposed tree roots, there will also be a very large brown trout. To move the fish the lure must be worked right in front of its nose; otherwise, the trout won't budge.

Sometimes, getting anything under a bank is impossible, but there is a tactic that sometimes provokes an attack. I prefer a large streamer and hefty fly rod, but any gear and lure will work. Cast the lure right to the bank. Bouncing off trees, dirt or rocks is fine and part of the game. As soon as the bait reaches the target, the line is stripped in as fast as possible, or the spinner retrieved very quickly. This is done over and over, literally pounding the banks, bushes or any cover you find.

Even on a very bright summer day, brown trout cannot resist this activity. They will come out of nowhere and race after your lure. More fish will be missed than hooked, but this can be some of the most exciting (and nerve wracking) trout fishing around. When you find a stretch of water that is deep, fast and with lots of cover, undercut banks (big fish will always be here) and submerged logs and brush, you have found brown trout heaven. Landing 50 percent of the trout you move is a good success rate.

Also, small streams, less than 20 feet wide, that flow into brown trout rivers nearly always hold big fish, especially in the fall. Look for the same water you would fish on a river and any protected deep hole. Browns will be there. Anglers take fish of several pounds in streams that are narrow enough to jump across in spots, but also have holes several feet deep for the browns to hide in. Depth, with several current seams distorting and refracting the light, equals cover.

More than any other trout, browns seek out overhead protection. With the notable exception of spawning time, or when they are feeding on a prolific insect hatch, browns will not be found out in the open like rainbows or cutthroat holding in the riffles. Browns are predators of secrecy and stealth.

Most anglers believe that browns fight with deep runs, and rainbows are the acrobats of the family. In cold rivers, I've found that most browns jump at least once and often several times when first hooked. Then, they run long and deep. If you are not ready for these initial jumps, the fish, more often than not, will slip the hook.

Big Browns In The Fall

In the fall, a great place to look for big browns, one that is a little easier to fish, is out in the open along gravel bars. This is the type of stream bottom the fish use for spawning. You won't find the fish here on bright days. They will be hiding under cover. But when the skies cloud over and the weather turns autumn nasty, large trout will move out over these areas.

Almost anything worked right along the bottom, bounced right up to the browns, will turn the trick, but a red-and-white spoon cast quartering upstream and then retrieved medium-fast as it swings across and in front of the fish produces vicious strikes more often than anything else. The fish will be large and 10-pound test or greater line (hefty by trout standards) is required along with a good ball-bearing swivel. Terminal tackle is the weak link in the equipment chain for most anglers and is responsible for more lost fish than any other piece of gear. A little attention and money spent here can increase catch rates by a third or more.

The most important thing to remember with browns is that the best time to fish for them during the summer is late in the day or at night. In autumn, after August, watch for cooling weather coupled with cloud cover. Whatever you use, make sure it is large. Spoons should weigh a quarter ounce or more. Streamers should be at least No. 4 and No. 2 is better still.

Finally, look for stretches of a river that have plenty of cover like brush piles and undercut banks. This cannot be stressed too often. In water with good numbers of browns, fish the banks first and hard.

That's where the big boys hang out.

Sea Trout Provide Great Sport

The sea-run or anadromous form of the brown trout is called the sea trout. They normally reach about 5 pounds in their East

When fishing a river with lots of brush and undercut banks for browns, work the banks first and hard. This stretch is ideal brown country, and the big ones hang out close to the banks where there is cover.

Complete Anglers Library

Coast spawning rivers. There are also minor populations in Argentina, Chile and New Zealand. In Europe, the fish is known variously as the peal, sewin, white trout, finnock, whitling and herling. The largest sea trout are caught in Argentina, Norway and Sweden where the fish may reach 30 pounds. Silvery in appearance when first returned from the ocean, the trout gradually darken and return to their freshwater appearance as they spend more time in native rivers.

The majority of sea trout spend the first three years of life in their home rivers before migrating to sea where some of the trout spend as little as two months before returning to freshwater. Biologists consider the sea trout/brown trout relationship to be the equivalent of the steelhead/rainbow trout relationship. It is believed that mature trout return after three years in the ocean while immature fish return after a year and a half to river estuaries. Mature fish weigh from 4 to 9 pounds, and immature fish weigh around 1 to 3 pounds.

Zane Grey said, "The fight of a sea trout is thus stronger than that of a brown trout and, if possible, even more active and full of quick turns ... I prefer a good fresh run sea trout of three or four pounds in a river on a single-handed rod and fine tackle to anything else." Fine praise indeed from a man who spent every spare minute fishing throughout the world.

The sea trout is a cautious individual and as such, easier to catch after dark when found in rivers. It is less spooky in lakes. Tactics that work on freshwater browns work on sea trout. When found in the mouths of rivers, sea trout are provoked by large streamers cast far out on the water and rapidly stripped through the water. The fish, when hooked, is famous for a leaping, fast-running fight.

3

Rainbow Trout

Should there be one species embodying all the characteristics an angler would want in a perfect freshwater
sportfish, the rainbow trout would have to be on
anyone's short list. Strong, beautiful, acrobatic, requiring skill to take consistently, inhabiting pure waters usually in
beautiful settings—basically the rainbow is a designer sportfish
perfect for a variety of fishing appetites.

The rainbow is native to North America with a natural
range of northern Mexico up into Alaska. You can catch the
fish in New York, Ontario, Wisconsin, South Dakota,
Wyoming, California—throughout the continent.

More rainbows are taken by anglers than any other species
of trout, and no other fish is raised and stocked as extensively
throughout the world. Rainbows are found in unlikely places
such as North Dakota, fee trout ponds outside of Cleveland or
at put-and-take lakes in Florida. This is the closest thing there
is to a universal trout (or gamefish for that matter).

Rainbows grow to exceptional size. One weighing over 52
pounds was taken from Jewel Lake, British Columbia. The
world record by an angler is 42 pounds, 2 ounces from Bell
Island in Alaska. The species takes its name from a red lateral
band that varies widely in intensity from deep, pink shading
toward red during spawning in some rivers to the faintest
suggestion of rose in certain lake-dwelling races. The coloring
of the gill plates will match the intensity and shading

Rainbows are legendary for their leaping abilities when hooked providing considerable excitement. This big rainbow was taken during the spawning season in 2 feet of water.

Rainbow Trout

of the lateral band. The rainbow can be anywhere from green to blue to olive-brown on its back. The flanks are usually silver and the belly is white. Stream dwellers tend to be heavily marked with black spots.

There are many subspecies, races and hybrids. Races of non-migratory rainbows include Eagle Lake, Arlee, Kamloops, Shasta, Kern River and Royal Silver. Rainbow eggs have been shipped to New Zealand, northern India, South Africa, Europe, Chile, Argentina, Japan and anywhere else anglers wander. The species readily cross-breeds or hybridizes with other salmonids including cutthroat and goldens, which produce a beautiful and feisty fish.

The rainbow resembles a cutthroat in some waters, but the two can be distinguished by the fact that the rainbow has no teeth on the back of its tongue (hyoid). In its anadromous or sea-run form (which will be discussed later in this chapter), the rainbow is known as a steelhead and spends a sizable portion of its life in the ocean or one of the Great Lakes before returning to its native stream to spawn.

Rainbows Are Spring Spawners

Rainbows are spring spawners. Spawning occurs from February through June for inland populations with those swimming in some cold-water lakes holding off until as late as August in isolated cases. The fish build redds, or nests, in the gravels of rivers and streams near the end of a pool or in inlet or outlet streams when occupying lake environments. If there is not any suitable spawning area in a given water, the females gradually reabsorb their eggs. Females lay roughly 1,000 eggs per pound of body weight. These eggs hatch within two months under normal conditions. Both male and female experience a large decline in weight following spawning—up to one-half the body weight in males. As a result, the fish provide poor sport for several weeks after this activity. At these times, the trout are dull in color, loose of flesh and anemic in behavior. Anglers have caught post-spawn 5-pound rainbows that have turned on their sides and come meekly to net as soon as they felt the bite of the hook, not a very energizing experience.

Rainbows live between seven and 12 years depending on the location. On the average, a 2-year-old rainbow is about 8 or 9

Rainbows are prevalent all along the western seaboard, through western Canada into Alaska. They're also found throughout East-Central states and throughout the Rockies.

inches, but in certain fertile lakes of the West, the species grows as much as an inch per month for the first two seasons, producing trout of 2 feet and 7 pounds or more.

Rainbows prefer the fast water sections of rivers and also cold-water lakes, ponds and reservoirs. Along with the rest of the trout family, they also thrive in spring-fed creeks.

There is not a more acrobatic fish in freshwater than a rainbow taken from fast current. In spring, while casting a spoon at lake inlets, you'll often find fish over 5 pounds coming out of nowhere and slamming down on the lure. Before an angler can collect himself, the rainbow has already torn into his line while tailwalking, crashing and leaping out into the lake. Clamping down to check the fish usually equals a break-off. There is no way to handle such a fish with lightweight gear. Big rainbows create heart-stopping experiences.

In lakes, large rainbows spin anglers in float tubes around. Big'bows fight anglers for 20 minutes or more before fraying the line and snapping free to safety. Pound for pound, river-run rainbows are the strongest of the trout, with browns coming in at a close second.

When fishing rivers and streams, with the intention of catching rainbows, look for moving water. It will usually be the

Rainbow Trout

fastest water you can find.

The species loves to feed in fast runs while holding down on shelves just above drop-offs into deep pools. The current may be racing along at the surface, but at the bottom (the benthic zone) surface drag between the streambed and the water reduces the flow to nearly zero. This is an ideal situation for big trout to hold in—little effort is expended, food passing overhead is visible yet the fish's presence is masked by the rippling currents staggered throughout the water column.

To appreciate the masking aspects of moving water, walk out on a bridge spanning a trout stream, one where there are visible trout holding below you. Pick out one fish and watch as it moves from side to side and slightly up and down stream while feeding. You will notice that as the trout moves underneath a seam where two differing speeds of water converge, a second or two is needed for your eyes to readjust and pick out the fish again. The same visual screen hampers predators flying overhead or prowling a bank. Cover as slight as this is the difference between a trout's life and death in a river.

Work Riffles On Sunny Days

A good place to prospect for rainbows during the height of a sunny day is in riffles, for the reasons mentioned above and because the water washes down plenty of aquatic insects. Usually these insects occur in nymphal form (nymphs are worm-like in appearance and spend as much as three years crawling along the stream bottom feeding on other insects and plant life before rising through the water to take flight and mate above the water).

Coupled with the rich oxygen content of the water, riffles are prime spots for rainbows. Spinners cast quartering upstream and retrieved fast enough to create the designed action often produce rainbows on every cast in good streams. Bait and nymph fly patterns drifted through these normally rocky bottoms also produce. Spoons tend to be rolled over in the current here, more often than not spooking the trout.

Often rainbows hold steadily in water that is a combination run/riffle—deep with slight rippling on the surface. The dark appearance of the water is an indication of depth, and the rippling tells you that the current is swift, maybe as much as 7

Fast runs and riffles such as this one on the Big Hole River in Montana are prime rainbow trout water. Rainbows tend to hold in deep water that has a slight rippling on the surface.

Rainbow Trout

miles per hour, moving over an uneven bottom. Once again, this is a perfect habitat with the prerequisites of current-induced cover, available food and plenty of oxygen. Of the major species of trout, only the cutthroat displays a similar preference for this type of water, but not to the extent the rainbow does.

To some degree, all trout are herbacious, meaning that a portion of their diet consists of plants (mainly algae and other aquatic plants). Rainbows make a greater use of this food source than any other trout (with the cutthroat again being closest in utilizing plants for food). Working any area with aquatic plants is obviously a good idea for this reason, and the fact that weedbeds are nurseries for aquatic insects such as caddis flies, mayflies and stone flies along with freshwater shrimp known as scuds also helps.

Working a nymph down through these channels nearly always turns up a good fish, but a sturdy leader is required to avoid breaking-off in the weeds. Bait such as worms drifted through these spots are just as effective. Spinners also work well, but require a fine touch and make for difficult, often frustrating fishing.

Because rainbows will take to the air, frequently jumping a couple of feet out of the water, maintaining tension on the line is difficult but necessary. If the fish gains too much slack, it can throw the hook or crash back down on the line, using its body weight to snap the slender connection. There is not much an angler can do when a large rainbow accelerates across the surface of the water except to reel in slack as fast as possible and raise and lower the rod to maintain a steady, firm pressure on the line and trout. Most rainbows gain their freedom while suspended in air, shaking their heads.

When seeking rainbows, the most important thing to look for is moving water—deep, fast runs; shelves at the heads of pools; riffles; and combination deep runs/riffles. Also, work any aquatic plant growth. Spinners are much better than spoons and wooden minnows in this kind of water. Nymphs and bright streamers work with a fly rod, and worms are the bait of choice.

Steelhead Are Sea-Run Rockets
Something wonderful happens to a rainbow trout when it takes leave of its native rivers and runs downstream to spend a

When is a rainbow not a rainbow? When it has been in deep water such as the ocean or the Great Lakes. Then, they're transformed into a stronger, bigger version, called a steelhead.

few months or even years in the big water—whether it be the Pacific Ocean or one of the Great Lakes. The trout return to the rivers of their birth larger and tremendously stronger than when they left. These silver rockets are known as steelhead.

For hordes of West Coast and Great Lakes anglers, there is only one sportfish worthy of their attention and this is the steelhead. A rainbow is an impressive fish, but a steelhead takes on the strength and power of a salmon, which when combined with the acrobatics associated with the rainbow becomes an awe-inspiring trout to say the least.

Unlike Pacific salmon, steelhead may return to spawn in their home waters more than once; whereas the salmon die shortly after spawning. There are two distinct races of steelhead—winter-run and summer-run. Steelhead are silver when they first enter the rivers, but gradually as they move upstream and near their spawning grounds they begin to darken and the red band appears. Sexual changes in their physiology are responsible for this transformation which also includes the development of a kype in males. They then resemble rainbows except that they are slimmer in body shape. The fish grow large, though the average range on the coast is somewhere between 6 and 15 pounds. In the rushing, isolated rivers of British Columbia, steelhead reach weights of around 40 pounds.

It is believed that these fish evolved from the rainbow after periods of geologic upheaval, such as the ice age and volcanic eruptions. They adapted to take advantage of new spawning and feeding habitat provided in the ocean. Whether or not steelhead feed while in freshwater is the source of much unresolved debate. They do lose a good portion of body weight at this time, but they also will hit sacks of eggs and patterns that imitate these eggs. No one really knows for sure at this time. They may also strike out of an instinct, that has reached a fever pitch during spawning, to defend territory.

Summer And Winter Races

Steelhead that enter the rivers in spring, summer and fall are known as summer-run. Those entering in late fall, winter and early spring are known as winter-run. On most rivers these two races, or strains, will spawn at approximately the same time, late winter and early spring. Steelhead that enter freshwater as immature fish but then mature in the following six months to a year are also known as "green" fish, while the winter runs are mature or "ripe." Strains imprinted with these characteristics and planted in the Great Lakes exhibit quite similar behavior.

The two strains of steelhead are distinct races that maintain racial integrity when it comes to selecting periods of freshwater residency and spawning. While the two races may enter a given river at the same time, there is no evidence that the races mix. The largest steelhead tend to appear in rivers at the end of a given run and winter-run fish are generally the biggest, though summer-run fish may reach 20 pounds.

Steelhead that have completed spawning and are returning

It's hard to believe that this rainbow could become a steelhead. However, it will turn silvery in color by the time it hits deep water but then when it returns to the river, it will regain its coloration.

downriver to the sea are known as kelts, a name for Atlantic salmon in a similar stage of their lives. The fish have lost much of their bright spawning color and will not regain a "healthy-looking" appearance until they have had the opportunity to feed in the ocean. Despite their appearances, both sexes are in relatively fine physical condition following spawning. Fishermen usually run into these fish in March and April, and many streams are closed at this time to protect the fish.

The main difference between fishing for steelhead on the Pacific Coast and along the Great Lakes is the size of the tributary. Coastal rivers like the Columbia are huge, a mile across in some spots, while those in the Midwest are much smaller. As an example, those in Door County in Wisconsin have good runs of fish approaching 20 pounds that provide excellent sport in streams sometimes no more than 25 feet wide and just a couple feet deep.

Steelheading Is Tough At Times

Steelhead fishing is one discipline (an appropriate term when you consider that it often takes hundreds, maybe thousands, of casts in wet, freezing weather before connecting with a fish) where knowing the precise location of the run in a river is not merely a convenience, it is an absolute necessity. The trout do not live year-round in the river. You cannot take the fish by merely working good-looking holding areas like you do for inland trout. Often, the steelhead are already upstream or still downriver staging before a big push upstream.

Any method that will take rainbow trout will work with steelhead, though the tackle used will be larger because of the nature of the rivers the fish return to.

Heavy spinning gear is needed to cast large spoons and wobbling plugs. A 7.5-foot spinning rod with 10-pound test line or an 8-foot baitcasting setup with 12-pound test are ideal. These will handle ⅜- to ¾-ounce lures. Spoons are often cast upstream into the deep races of a river and retrieved while they run along the bottom and then finally swing in the current. Wobbling plugs work best when they are allowed on the retrieve to slowly drift in the current which produces a fluttering action. Fluorescent colors seem to work better than regular ones for this fishing. Drift spinners are a West Coast favorite. They are available in bright colors. These lures have propeller-like rubber wings that spin the lure on a wire shaft and are used by both trollers and drift fishers in larger rivers.

As with any trout fishing, spinners produce with steelhead, but they must be in large sizes and include fluorescent colors—both weighted and unweighted. Another good choice is a marabou jig, both because it easily sinks to the depth of the fish and does not often snag.

Spoons of from an inch to 3 inches in plain and hammered brass or silver along with those with streaks of red or white or a red-and-white finish also work well.

Spawn And Yarn Works Well

Many natural baits are used for steelhead, and they include shrimp, single eggs, night crawlers and salmon or steelhead spawn mixed with yarn.

When using the spawn-yarn method, baitholder hooks with barbs on the shanks that prevent the snell from reaching the hook eye work best. The loop of leader that lies between the hook eye and snell is slipped over the bait to hold it in place.

Spawn And Yarn Rig

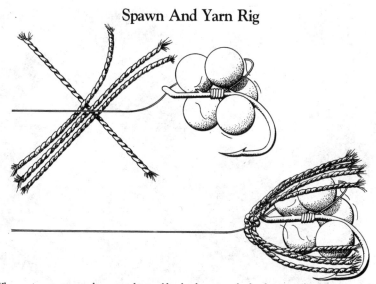

When using spawn and yarn, a loop of leader between the hook eye and snell is slipped over the bait to hold it in place. The yarn acts as a simple fly tied directly on the leader above the hook. To tie it, lay a 3-inch piece of fluorescent tying yarn on a flat surface and cross it with the leader. Lay three, 1½-inch strands of yarn over the leader and the tying yarn. Gather the tying yarn ends and tie a square knot, sliding this to the hook eye. Trim strands even.

The yarn, which acts as a simple but effective fly, is tied directly on the leader above the hook. This is done by laying a 3-inch piece of fluorescent tying yarn on a flat surface and crossing it with the leader. Over the leader and opposite the tying yarn, lay three, inch-and-a-half strands of yarn. Gather the tying yarn ends and tie a square knot, sliding this to the hook eye and trimming the strands so they are even.

When drift fishing, you must experiment with the amount of weight until the fly, bait or lure is just barely bouncing along the bottom, most often with a 3/16-inch-diameter pencil lead attached by running the line through a small hole drilled in the head of the weight. This line should be lighter in weight than the casting line so if snagged only the lead breaks off saving an expensive lure. The easiest method to adjust this weight is to attach six inch sections which can be cut to the desired weight to match given stream conditions. Surgical tubing slipped over the ring of a three-way swivel and cinched above the ring with nylon thread keeps the setup from twisting around the main line and itself. Just slip the lead into the tubing.

For the fly fisher, at least a 9-foot rod that can handle a

This 13-inch rainbow fell victim to a spinner. When the fish comes to the surface, the angler can fully expect a display of jumping that will be entertaining as well as rewarding.

minimum of a 7-weight line is required. Better still is a 9½-footer for 8 and 9-weight lines, preferably shooting heads that allow the angler to add distance necessary to reach holding areas on larger rivers.

A good example of a hand-tied steelhead leader, for fly fishing would be one with 40 inches of 25-pound test, 34 of 20, 8 of 15, 8 of 12 and 18 of 10. Another slightly lighter leader would consist of 38 inches of 25, 32 of 20, six each of 15, 12 and 10, and 20 inches of 8-pound test.

There are many patterns for steelhead. Some of the more popular ones include the Orange Shrimp, Umpqua, Skykomish Yellow, Stilliguamish Sunrise, Royal Coachman, Skunk, Kalama Special and Admiral.

Whatever method is chosen to be used for these fish, it only takes the feel and sight of one steelhead as it rockets across the water and then powers straight up a mighty rapid to hook the angler for life.

4

Brook Trout

The only sight prettier than that of a wild brook trout leaping above the surface of a tree-lined sapphire-colored pool would have to be a brace of brookies high above the water.

All trout are beautiful and the golden trout is just flat out spectacular, but a brookie in full spawning dress brings home with a colorful vengeance all of the reasons for chasing trout.

These trout have green-black backs highlighted with lighter wavy lines (vermiculations). Blood-red or even purple spots are splattered across the sides of the brook trout, and these dots are surrounded by sky-blue aureoles. The flanks of the fish give way subtly from green to yellow and then blazing orange that is almost red in autumn's spawning males. A line of black separates this riot of color from a perfectly white belly. The fish's fins are also bright orange or red, divided by black and then dipped in white. Spawning males are distinguished from the females by a kype and, often, a pronounced, humped back.

To see a fish such as this arching over a clean, burbling brook in fall with the aspens blasting yellow into a sharp blue sky is almost enough to make a person forget fishing. Almost. Feeling the fish's pull the end of your line and then holding this perfection in your hands complete the experience.

Brookie Is A True Native

The brook trout (Salvelinus fontinalis) is a true North

This large beaver pond produces many big brookies during fall spawning, especially along the point where the golden larch (pines), reflected in the almost still water, march to the shore.

Brook Trout   47

American native that is found down south in Georgia, up north near the Arctic Circle and way out west in Washington and Oregon, not to mention the far-flung reaches of the Canadian provinces, South America and Europe. And in the maritime possessions of Canada and down below the equator in Argentine waters, the trout exceed 30 inches and a dozen pounds more frequently than is healthy to ponder for any length of time. Beautiful, big-fish madness lurks in unexplored still waters running deep and undisturbed.

In Maine, the South and the Midwest, a 2-pounder is a trophy. In western states like Montana and Wyoming, 6 pounds is bragging size. As with most fish, the best brook trout water is also the most difficult to reach and is usually quite large—big lakes, brawling rivers. In Labrador, on some of the finest rivers, many of the most productive "pools" are a half-mile or more long. Big brook trout are extremely susceptible to angling pressure, so once they are discovered by anglers, the time of trophy fishing is limited to a matter of just a few seasons.

Before the onrushing development associated with "civilization," the brook trout was the only species of trout fly fishers chased in the eastern United States. Then, as numbers declined and the brown trout became established as a European substitute, the brookie declined in popularity in the late 19th century. Some of the reasons for this were the facts that browns grew larger more quickly, and also, because they were somewhat of a novelty.

The tiger trout is a cross between a brook and brown trout. The cross has the brook's vermiculations and the brown's coloring. This cross has an extremely aggressive disposition, but unfortunately only about one-third of the young are able to develop fully because of a disease inherent in the sac-fry. This cross rarely occurs in nature and is unable to naturally reproduce because it is a salmonid mule (sterile adult). The hybrid is an excellent quarry for the dry fly fisherman.

Brook trout have experienced a resurgence in popularity and today thrive in streams, rivers, lakes, ponds—anywhere with clean, cold water. In some mountain lakes, the fish do so well and are present in such great numbers that they become stunted, hammer-handled specimens. Many lakes in the West have limits of 30 or more fish per angler per day and even with

The main areas for brook trout are throughout the central and northern Rockies, as well as the Northeast and eastern Canada.

heavy fishing pressure, trout numbers remain high and constant. Unfortunately, these trout are often big-headed and skinny-bodied.

Brook trout spawn from September in the northern limits of their range on through December in the southernmost regions. A 6-inch fish will lay at the most 200 eggs, but 15-inch females will produce well over 1,000. The trout construct redds in areas of good flow, especially around upwelling springs. They will spawn in extremely small brooks. However, in lakes, their demands are not as rigid, and a nest can be located in either shallow or deep water.

Brook trout may live 10 years, but a 6-year-old fish is 1-in-10,000. And despite the ability of the trout to reproduce in astounding numbers, brookies are more susceptible to warm water temperatures than any of the major trout species. These fish seem to grow best where predators exist in healthy numbers. Other species are needed as a natural means of brook trout population control. Some of the best brookie water also produces trophy northern pike and extremely large walleyes. Farther north, lake trout and arctic char keep the populations down to manageable levels through predation.

When the fish are reared in hatcheries, even with breeding

among normally-colored fish, albino trout occur with some small degree of regularity. The fish are more orange than pink and the eyes may be black or pink. Albinos in the wild are an extreme rarity for the obvious reason that they are easy to spot by predators.

Brook trout are related to lake trout, arctic char and bull trout. In many Western rivers and tributaries where both brook and bull trout are present, hybridization is a common occurrence. In fact, the introduction of brookies in the West is a major reason for the decline of pure-strain native populations of bull trout.

Beaver Ponds Mean Brook Trout

When fishing for brook trout, one type of water comes to mind that is indelibly linked with the species—beaver ponds. Sure, other species make use of this fabricated environment, but at nowhere near the extent of the squaretail. You can take brookies in dammed-up mosquito-infested bogs in northern Wisconsin, in small rodent-designed ponds hiding behind thickets of tag alder in world-class grizzly country in northwest Montana and in charming little lakes sitting in alpine meadows way up in the mountain passes of Colorado. Wherever a beaver can block or hinder the progress of water as it obeys its gravitational downhill imperative, you will find brook trout, often in great numbers and of surprisingly large dimensions considering the fact that many ponds are less than an acre in surface area. These waters are rich in nutrients and, as a result, filled with aquatic insects along with larger bait such as leeches, crayfish, and small frogs.

The best beaver pond for the angler is a new or relatively new one. The older the impoundment, the more silt and debris that has accumulated on the bottom. The fate of all beaver ponds is to eventually turn into swamps, then grassy meadows—eutrophication is the name of the process. A 2-year-old beaver pond is prime stuff, worthy of serious investigation with a red-and-white spoon in the $\frac{1}{16}$th or $\frac{1}{8}$th-ounce range cast with an ultra-light rig and 2-pound (4-pound maximum) line.

The delicate setup allows you to thoroughly work the water without causing a trout stampede to deep cover. And a 1-pound

Brook trout will readily take spinners, especially chartreuse, as this fish has just done. Look for them in lakes along edges of weedbeds surrounding pockets of clear water.

brookie provides superb sport on this gear. Spinners work, but not like the red-and-white spoon which has been a classic, dependable trout lure over the years.

The pond needs to be approached with stealth, maybe in a crouch, and you might have to use bankside bushes for cover. If trout are rising and feeding on surface insects, cast well beyond them and bring the spoon through the pond with a steady retrieve. If feeding fish are not in evidence, cast to brushy banks, just behind the dam itself, up into any inlets and across any visible channels. The trout's coloration is ideal for blending into this environment. Water that at first appears barren, may hold hundreds of brookies who cannot be caught until the sun is behind the pines and shadows cover the water. Only then will the fish venture out into the open to feed.

Perhaps even more than the brown trout, the brookie is a creature of dawn and dusk. The fish are curious, but easily spooked and extremely cautious. Aggressive browns and rainbows are frequently observed at midday, but this behavior is almost nonexistent in squaretails who prefer the overhead security that deepening shadows on the water provide.

Brook Trout   51

Brook trout are among the most beautiful of the trout species, and this 1½-pounder is a truly fine example of the species. This brookie moved out into the open to feed and was caught.

Look For Springs In Lakes

One last location that is good water for all trout, but especially so for brookies, is found in lakes. During the heat of summer when the water begins to reach uncomfortable levels for the brookies, the fish seek out springs shooting forth life-saving streams of cold water from beneath the lake bed. Finding these trout magnates is difficult, but one tip is to look for pockets of open water in among aquatic weed growth.

On a chain of lakes such as those found on the large river systems of Ontario, finding brook trout is difficult work in July until you cast a spinner over the edge of a bed of lily pads into clear water sometimes no more than 5 feet in diameter. A good fish will often hit the lure immediately, before it has dropped even a couple of inches.

A thermometer will indicate that the water in the center of this pool is often 15 degrees cooler than the water surrounding the opening.

Similar pockets nearly always hold at least one and often three or four trout and each location reveals itself to the thermometer to be a cold-water spring. The brookies here are commonly over a pound and up to 3 pounds. Big, dominant fish take the choice spots in a diminishing environment. This type of diminishing environment normally turns up fish during the dog days of summer.

The things to remember with brook trout are to fish any beaver-dam ponds or lakes, look for isolated, big-drainage systems and fish any springs you discover in lakes.

5

Cutthroat Trout

When you live in the Rocky Mountains and someone mentions native trout, you think of cutthroat trout and none other—not rainbows, not Dolly Varden, not bull trout and certainly not browns or brooks.

True, the cutthroat trout, especially the feisty sea-run strain, is also associated with the lush, green rain forests of the Pacific Coast. But, when many of us think of this species images of mountain lakes beneath ice-scoured glacial cirques above timberline come fondly to mind; or crashing, rushing mountain torrents spilling down over boulders and through tangles of downed larch and fir; or finally, big rivers like the Yellowstone rolling away between spectacular mountain peaks in the Paradise Valley.

The fish gets its name from the orange to scarlet slashes running laterally below the lower jaw. The back of the trout can be anywhere from green to blue to black. Black spots can be scattered throughout the length of the body or concentrated near the tail section. The flanks of the cutthroat can range from silver to yellowish-green to bright red on spawning males. The lower fins are often orange.

The range of the species is from Prince William Sound in Alaska down through northern California and throughout the inland western U.S. and Canada. The fish resembles the rainbow, a species with which the cutthroat frequently

High mountain lakes are perfect water for cutthroat trout which often are seen rising in deep water. No other trout is more closely identified with this type of wilderness.

Cutthroat Trout   55

Cutthroat trout can be found throughout the Rockies and along the West Coast from northern California to Alaska.

cross-breeds. When this happens the rainbow's characteristics remain mostly intact with the exception that the "cuts" or slashes are present, often in orange. The cutthroat also cross-breeds with the golden trout, retaining most of its markings while taking on a pronounced golden sheen along its sides and gill covers.

Numerous Subspecies Exist

One of the unique aspects of the cutthroat is that where the species is isolated as a result of geologic formations, in other words, separated from other cutthroats by mountain ranges or even deserts, the fish takes on distinct physical characteristics that are endemic to a specific region. Fourteen subspecies of cutthroat have been identified. These subspecies include the coastal, westslope, Yellowstone, Snake River, Lahontan (a threatened species that has adapted to highly-alkaline desert lakes and grows to very impressive sizes), Humboldt, Paiute, Alvord Lake basin, Willow/Whitehorse Creek, Bonneville, Colorado River, greenback (threatened), Rio Grande and the yellowfin (now extinct).

The cutthroat spawns in mid- to late-winter along the Pacific Coast into early summer in the mountain West. The fish live 10 years, but this is an exception with six years a more reasonable life span. The largest cutthroat was a Lahontan specimen taken from Pyramid Lake in Nevada weighing 41 pounds. In the mountain waters, a fish of 3 pounds or more is an exceptional trout and sea-run average about 5 pounds or a little less. In high-mountain streams, the fish are much smaller with a 12-incher a true trophy.

Perhaps no other member of the water-quality-sensitive trout clan is more affected by changes for the worse in its environment than the cutthroat. The westslope cutthroat has disappeared from all but a dozen or so of its native streams on the Flathead National Forest in northwest Montana as a result of logging and the introduction of rainbow trout years ago. Extensive work by state Department of Fish, Wildlife and Parks fisheries biologists seems to indicate that the trout can be re-established in its original watersheds, provided no additional threats to its habitat occur and stream bank habitat is restored in clearcut areas.

Cutthroat Prefer Smaller Food Sources

The cutthroat has a reputation for being easy to catch and a poor fighter. There is some truth to both of these traits, but the trout is still a worthy adversary, if for no other reason than chasing a cutthroat allows an angler to spend time in some of the most beautiful and wild country in North America.

Where big browns are associated with eating forage fish and smaller trout, cutthroats feed predominately on aquatic insects, terrestrials like grasshoppers, crickets and ants and on freshwater shrimp. Imitations of these food sources are the best bets for catching cutthroats and that is why these fish are more a fly fisher's quarry. The comparative large size of plugs, spoons and spinners often spook cutthroats before they have a chance to consider what it is they are fleeing from.

One of the reasons cutthroats are easy to catch is that they are usually found in remote regions that receive little pressure. A cutthroat's susceptibility to the wiles of an angler, particularly if dry flies are used, is more a result of provinciality than stupidity. Anyone who has fished for the Yellowstone cutthroat in Yellowstone Park understands this situation. Park trout are often taken a half-dozen times or more in a season by the hordes

Cutthroats, usually found in the higher mountains, are smaller than their cousins. Any fish over a pound is a good catch. This West Slope species is common to the northern Rockies.

of anglers that descend on this over-publicized trout Mecca. A fish that survives for more than four years has probably been pulled from the water a few times. When you see cutthroats of between 2 feet and 30 inches delicately sipping tiny insects on a river's surface, your heart races and your hands shake. Only the most delicate of offerings, one that perfectly matches what is hatching before you, tied to the slenderest of tippets, will fool these fish. And if you do manage to touch one, good luck holding it on the spiderweb-like leader.

Cutthroat are not acrobatic fish, but any one of them weighing more than a few pounds will put up a strong, below-surface struggle. This is especially so in rivers where the trout instinctively make use of their bodies by running sideways in the current, gaining power from the force of the water pushing against their muscular flanks.

For the fly fisherman, one of the best patterns around for the small mountain streams is the Goddard Caddis No. 14 to No. 18. This high-floating deerhair pattern will nearly always draw the cutthroat out from beneath the logjams that is probably its species-specific habitat. Find a logjam and you will

Complete Anglers Library

find cutthroat, but the big ones hold way under the debris and sinking a nymph or wet fly under this stuff is difficult. (So is pulling a hefty trout out of a hole like this.)

Small spinners ($\frac{1}{24}$ and $\frac{1}{16}$ ounce) of silver, brass or copper with undressed hooks will also take cutthroat consistently in pools and when cast quartering downstream and slowly retrieved. A small, wriggling worm worked through the jams and pools can be deadly, too.

Cutthroat, more than most trout, feed in a definite path, especially in high mountain lakes. Standing on the shore you can watch them, often in pairs, work their way down toward you as they dine on emerging aquatic insects. This makes anticipating where to cast a dry fly or small spinner relatively easy. The fish will race to take the offering provided it is presented with some degree of caution.

The main difference between sea-run cutthroat and steelhead seems to be that the cutthroat are taken more frequently in estuaries, especially when the tide turns and begins to run upriver. Streamers and wet flies worked along the swirls of upwelling current produce trout.

Fishing for cutthroat is a straight-forward proposition. Look for unspoiled, pristine streams or lakes. Fish any logjams thoroughly and use small flies or spinners.

6

Golden Trout

Ask anyone who claims to know anything about salmonids, "What is the most beautiful trout?" Nine times out of 10 the answer will be "golden trout." While each species has its admirers, goldens are magnificent fish. The largest ones are often taken from small streams that connect lake chains 11,000 feet above sea level many miles back in the Wind River Mountains of Wyoming's Bridger Wilderness.

There you can sometimes see dozens of the fish holding in pools below small waterfalls. Casting a weighted Muddler Minnow in front of these fish produces a savage, territorial response; the fish are preparing to spawn and any interloper is an unwanted visitor. The golden will immediately race down through shallow riffles and over cascades before you finally catch it. Holding the trout in your hands, you admire the technicolor beauty. The sides are blaze orange, hot pink and blood red as are the belly and the fins that are also tipped in white. The back shades to gold, then yellow, then green and dark spots mark the dorsal fin running down through the tail. There is a slight hump to the male's back and a large kype. The golden is definitely ready to spawn.

The Wind River region probably has more golden trout lakes than anywhere else in the world and plenty of very large goldens swim there. The Bighorn Mountains to the east also have nice goldens as do Montana's Beartooths to the north.

Golden trout are a wildly colored fish normally found in high mountain lakes and streams. Any golden over 2 pounds is a trophy, but it will put up a fight disproportionate to its size.

Goldens Native To Sierra Range

Goldens originated in the Kern River drainage of the Sierra Mountains in central California, and the stock was exported throughout the inland West and as far away as England before the state passed legislation prohibiting the shipping of eggs and fish out of California.

Idaho, Montana, Washington and Wyoming still carry out stocking programs. Small populations hold out in the Uinta Mountains of Utah and the Pincher Creek area of Alberta. The fish may be swimming in a few isolated lakes in Colorado and Oregon, also.

There is a common misconception that the species can only survive in high altitude lakes and streams many thousands of feet above sea level. In fact, the golden will do quite well in any

Golden Trout

cold-water lake that is suitable for rainbows or brooks or cutthroats. The problem is that most state fish and game departments have already established viable populations of other species in appropriate waters and cannot find any places to stock goldens. The fish readily hybridizes with cutthroats for one thing. Goldens also live around 10 years under ideal conditions, and the world record for the species is 11 pounds taken from Cooks Lake in Wyoming in 1948. Rumors persist of fish approaching 15 pounds in Montana and Wyoming and reliable reports from a fisheries biologist describes one golden of over 12 pounds.

The desirability of goldens led to their being transplanted from their original waters in California to neighboring lakes and streams in the 1870s, often in pails, coffee cans or in anything that would hold water and the fish.

One story has it that in 1876 a Colonel Stevens lugged a dozen of the fish from Mulkey Creek in the Sierra over a high pass and dumped them in Cottonwood Creek. The Colonel operated a sawmill in the area, and the goldens were stocked for his recreation. In 1918, the California Department of Fish and Game began raising the trout in the Cottonwood Lakes whose elevation is 11,000 feet. Today, eggs are still gathered from those lakes and transported to the Mt. Whitney hatchery before being planted in various wilderness lakes.

Several subspecies of goldens exist including the Salmo whitei and Salmo gilberti in Coyote Creek; Salmo roosevelti of Volcano Creek; and Salmo roosevelti in the Culver Lakes drainage. All of these trout are differentiated by minor variations in color and marking, but as Robert H. Smith says in his book, Native Trout of North America, trying to compare them is "like trying to compare two sunsets."

Nobody knows for sure the evolutionary history of goldens, but some experts believe the species may be descendants of redband trout, of which rare members like the Gila and Mexican golden are members.

There are several theories based on why goldens evolved into the brightly-colored fish we find swimming in various lakes and streams today.

First, their colors tend to mirror the environment of their native range, the red rocks and many-colored gravels of the

Goldens are found primarily in higher locations in the Rockies and parts of California and Washington.

Kern Basin, making the fish difficult to spot by predators. Another reason may be that the brightest-colored males are more attractive to spawning females, and this intense coloring may communicate a willingness to defend territory to other males. This seems to hold true with the trout observed in the Bridger Wilderness. The most colorful males also were the ones that struck streamers most readily and pods of darker females clustered around these males more frequently than with smaller, less-colored males.

An interesting theory holds that severe light, unfiltered by the atmosphere at high elevations, presents deadly levels of solar radiation, and the goldens' color scheme may actually be a form of protection. Some credence is given this theory because the trout lose much of their color intensity when moved to lower-elevation lakes.

Feeding Patterns Are Sporadic

Golden trout are legendary for their off-and-on feeding habits. There are times when absolutely nothing will interest the fish, and there are times when the water seems to boil with their feeding. The best an angler can do is to bring both a spinning rod and a fly rod (live bait has never seemed to be very effective on goldens, and considering the rarity of this species, artificials are less likely to injure fish that should be returned to the water after being netted) when a trip is made far back and high up in seldom-visited golden country.

For the spin fisherman, ¼-ounce and smaller spoons and spinners work best on ultra-light gear with 4-pound-test line. To help avoid spooking the fish, the lighter the gear the better. Silver and gold for both, along with red-and-white and then black-and-white on both the spoons and spinner blades are the most productive finishes. Some anglers familiar with goldens claim chartreuse on a spinner's body works well.

For the fly fisher, a 6-weight rod of 8 ½ feet is adequate. Dries like the Adams, Royal Wulff, Mosquito and Goddard Caddis for fast water are good selections in sizes No. 10 to No. 18. Olive woolly worms, Muddler Minnows, Zonkers and Girdle Bugs cover the streamer action in No. 2 through No. 8. Nymphs should include Hare's ears, Zug bugs, Golden stones and Princes from No. 12 to No. 18.

On lakes, the best locations are off from points, along rock walls and along drop-offs next to where snowslides tumble into the water bringing unearthed insects with them. Casting and then letting a spinner or spoon sink near the bottom will sometimes bring up goldens. When they are rising on the surface, determine their direction and cast well ahead of them. Then, retrieve the lure at a medium pace. If the goldens are cooperative, they will strike quickly, but more often than not they will follow the lure almost to the rod tip. This is frustrating, to say the very least, when the fish is one of several pounds or more.

With flies you also cast well ahead of the anticipated feeding course, letting the pattern rest for several seconds and then twitching it slightly to attract the golden's attention. Sometimes, when the trout are finicky, a woolly worm cast out on the surface and allowed to slowly sink will produce fish. Do not apply any motion here or you will spook any trout within 50 feet. Goldens normally inhabit gin-clear waters and have good eyesight, so caution and stealth are always in order.

When the goldens are moving in the streams, usually up from inlets, a spinner, spoon or streamer worked directly in front of the holding trout will take them. The goldens will,

Complete Anglers Library

Drop-offs along the ends of points or where snow slides tumble into the water attract goldens that are foraging for insects and baitfish. Spoons and streamers work well, as does live bait.

many times, bat the offering out of the way with their snouts, but after perhaps as many as two dozen casts, the fish will often attack the lure or streamer to eliminate the intrusion. The fight, at times like this, is always spirited and you can take a number of fish from the same group because they are so focused on spawning that the disturbance from playing the fish is only a momentary diversion.

Just remember that goldens are under stress at this period, and they should be played quickly and then carefully revived and released. A large female can represent a sizable proportion of that year's breeding population. In these fragile, alpine lakes and streams, goldens are an extremely rare resource that need to be fished with care and concern by the angler.

So, to catch goldens, look for points, rock walls, drop-offs

Many golden lakes are above timberline such as this one in Wyoming's Bridger Wilderness at 11,000 feet. Persistence pays off as goldens often will ignore offerings before finally taking the bait.

and any other physical structure in lakes. Spoons and spinners along with streamers work best in both lakes and streams. Woolly worms often work when nothing else will. However, the angler must be prepared to experiment to find the right combination so as not to wind up with nothing to show for his work.

Traveling into golden country is a treat in itself, because the lakes and rivers are always in unspoiled mountain surroundings. This is fortunate for the angler, because fishing solely for goldens can often be a frustrating, fishless experience. This is the time to savor the beauty of the pristine lakes and the majestic mountains which ring the goldens' home.

7

Lake Trout

L ake trout are the largest member of the freshwater trout family in North America as they can reach weights of 100 pounds or more. Really a char, the species is also known as a togue in the eastern U.S., Mackinaw in the West and gray trout in Canada. Anglers throughout the world seek this fish not so much because of its fighting qualities, but because of the large size it attains.

Rarely are lake trout found anywhere but in cold, clear, well-oxygenated and very deep lakes, sometimes at depths of greater than 500 feet. River-dwelling populations do exist in waters that empty into large lakes in Alaska, Labrador and northern Quebec and a few other locations. Lake trout are distributed throughout Canada, the Great Lakes, New England and scattered about the West with some trophy populations in western Montana. The range of this fish coincides with the land area covered by late Pleistocene glaciation.

The lake trout is the only freshwater species ranging into Alaska and northern Canada that does not also extend across the Bering Sea into Siberia. Many biologists believe that the taimen (Hucho taimen) which is native to the Volga and Russian Arctic drainages and the lake trout are descended from the same ancestor that crossed over the Bering gap in early or pre-Pleistocene times. Similarities between the species are far greater than the differences.

The body of the lake trout is normally silver-gray ranging

Trolling large lures like flatfish down deep, over 100 feet, will take lake trout such as this one when using heavy gear. A downrigger setup ensures that you're putting the bait where the fish are.

Lake Trout

through blue-gray and copper-green with pale spotting on the flanks, back, dorsal, adiposal and caudal fins. Lake trout have forked tails which is one of the best ways to tell them apart from the splake, a hybrid produced by crossing brook and lake trout whose name is derived from speckled trout and lake trout. The splake differs from other salmonid hybrids in that it is fertile and able to reproduce in the wild. The cross has the spotting of the lake trout and the basic coloration of the brook. The splake matures faster than the lake trout and averages larger than the brook and substantially smaller than the lake. The hybrid is most frequently taken by trolling in similar fashion as that employed for lake trout.

While these fish do reach 100 pounds, a 40-pounder is a big fish for any angler, and the world record is 65 pounds. Fish over 20 years old are not uncommon and the species matures in four to 10 years.

Lake Trout Are Fall Spawners

Gravel or rocky lake bottoms in water often over 100 feet deep are prime spawning areas for lake trout in the Great Lakes, but in shallow lakes they may be found in shoals. The area is swept clean by the fish, but a redd is not constructed as with other trout species. This activity takes place from late August well into December, and each site has several males and females participating as the eggs and milt are scattered across the bottom. The eggs are extremely susceptible to predation from smaller lake trout, other trout species, suckers and perch.

The lamprey eel so decimated adult lake trout populations in the Great Lakes that the commercial catch of trout plummeted from 7.5 million pounds in 1946 to 385,000 in 1960. Control of lamprey populations and aggressive re-introduction programs for the lake trout are gradually returning this excellent gamefish back to its thriving, historical population levels of the mid 1900s.

Young fish feed on insects, terrestrials and freshwater shrimp and other crustaceans. Adult fish feed on whitefish, kokanee, other trout, sculpins and many other forage fish.

In the species' southern range, it is usually found near the bottoms of lakes except in late fall, winter and early spring when surface waters are quite cold. In the northern range where

Head north if you want to find lake trout. Most of the prime areas in north-central and northeastern United States or the West Slope of the Rockies and throughout Canada and much of Alaska.

lake temperatures on the surface remain cold throughout the year, lake trout can be found at any depth.

Trolling Is Most Popular Method

Lake trout can be taken by spinning, fly fishing and baitcasting, but by far the most popular and effective method is trolling down deep with downriggers and using heavy balled weights and large spoons and plugs.

Fish locators and solid knowledge of local structure and temperature levels throughout the water column are a must for those who seek deepwater lakers. Without this local knowledge, an angler definitely should avail himself of the services of a local guide for the first few outings. This is the only "quick" way to learn the water sufficiently to begin to fish on your own.

On many lakes, flatfish are the lure of choice and only the largest sizes are used. T-60s that are 6 inches long with a pair of heavy-duty treble hooks are trolled, often at depths of 200 feet, through schools or past individual fish indicated by a fish locator. Downriggers or lead-core line are used to submerge the lure to the proper depth. More often than not, if the flatfish is trolled past the trout, it will take. However, just as often the fight is somewhat of a disappointment as the fish is unable to

Lake Trout

Taking to the big lakes, particularly the Great Lakes, in search of trout should be treated like going out onto the ocean. A properly outfitted boat that can handle large swells from rapidly changing weather makes the quest more fun for the fishermen.

cope with the abrupt changes in pressure as it is hauled up rapidly through the depths.

Another problem in some northern Canadian lakes such as Great Slave, Great Bear and Athabasca is getting a spoon you are casting through a layer of northern pike that commonly hold at shallower depths than the trout. The northerns are so numerous that frustrated anglers find themselves taking the pike on every cast without being able to reach the depth where the lakers are holding.

When the trout congregate at inlets, they can be taken by casting along the edges of the river current as it plays out into the lake. Big spoons, spinners, flatfish and large streamers for the fly fisher retrieved quickly through the water will take fish regularly. Large bait such as smelt, which lake trout feed on extensively, drifted along the bottom in these locations also will bring in fish.

For the angler planning to fish this species without guidance, there are two choices. The first is to inquire locally about where to fish and then follow others out onto the lake and fish in the general vicinity. However, a fish locator is an absolute must. The other option is to fish river inlets in lakes with proven populations of the species. Working these areas beginning in late summer and running through autumn with large spoons, flatfish and spinners or big, weighted streamers is the best bet. The baitfisher should try smelt or similar bait, weighted and drifted along the bottom where the current of the river is visible as it enters the lake.

8

Other Trout

Although most of the waters NAFC members find near home commonly contain one or more of the trout species discussed earlier in this book, a number of species of salmonid can be expected to be encountered sooner or later, if you pursue trout seriously. These "other trout" are typically found in more remote areas, but within their restricted range they often seem to occur in plentiful numbers.

Arctic Char

Similar to the brook trout in appearance, this char is also related to bull trout, lake trout and Dolly Varden. Because the fish is often found in brook trout waters in eastern Canada, the two are frequently confused with each other by many inexperienced anglers.

The arctic char is found throughout cold waters of the northern hemisphere ranging from northern Canada, to Baffin Island, Greenland, Iceland, northern Norway, northern Siberia and Alaska in both sea-run and landlocked forms. The landlocked form also is common south of these regions in Norway, Sweden, Finland, England, Ireland, Scotland, west-central Europe and the USSR.

The char is differentiated from the brook trout by the lack of vermiculations and is not heavily spotted like other trout. When spots are present they are usually pink, orange or red.

Tracking the "exotic" varieties of trout, as these two anglers are doing, can be an exhilerating experience, considering the scenic areas that are home for them.

Other Trout

The flanks of the fish are often bright orange or red. Like other anadromous fish, they are silver when returning from the sea, gradually darkening as they spend more time in freshwater. An 8-pound landlocked fish is a trophy, but sea-runs of 25 pounds are taken occasionally. The world record is just slightly below 33 pounds.

The fish usually head down to the ocean at ice-out in late-spring or early summer, ascending in late-summer or early fall. They are about six years old when they begin this behavior and specimens of 30 years or more have been recorded. They do not remain long in saltwater and return to their rivers in large schools that are visible by the rolling and jumping of the fish. These fish move in groups up a river, so an angler must spend a good deal of time finding them if they are not readily apparent at river mouths where they typically stage.

The species feeds on smaller fish, crustaceans and eels, with insects being an insignificant portion of its diet. Brightly-colored fly patterns worked through shallow tributary streams or riffles and runs will take char effectively. The fish fight best when from the sea and their sporting qualities fall off rapidly as they progress upstream. Steelhead patterns like the Thor and Golden Demon along with the Gray Ghost and Bloody Butcher are extremely effective.

The arctic char is often taken on lightweight spinning gear rigged with ¼- to ½-ounce spoons and spinners. Larger lures will take char, but the fish normally inhale the lure, and the resulting injury makes them poor sport on heavier gear.

This fish is an important food source for Inuits and the flesh can be anywhere from bright-red to off-white. One important thing to remember is that the arctic char resides in world-class bug country. As an angler once said after a recent trip to the Arctic, "I could barely see the fish through the clouds of hungry, biting mosquitoes."

Arctic Grayling

Grayling is one of the most unusual of the salmonids with its large, sail-like dorsal fin used for maneuvering in the swift currents found in its native waters. The biggest fish, nearly 6 pounds in rare instances, are found in places like the Northwest Territories, Alaska, British Columbia, Alberta, Manitoba and

Arctic grayling are defined by their prominent dorsal fin with turquoise spots. With the exception of large scales, graylings have the same look as their cousins, the trout family.

Saskatchewan. In the lower 48, Montana, Wyoming, Utah and Idaho have fishable populations, chiefly in higher-elevation lakes where grayling hit on bait, spinners and flies.

The species survived the ice age in waters that ran right up to the edges of the huge glaciers. Over the millennia they have evolved into an elongated, muscular shape that is perfect for the fast water they prefer.

The distinctive dorsal fin has irregular rows of turquoise spots, and occasionally, the upper edge is tinged with white or pink. The body of the fish leans toward dark silver to a purplish cast with discernible scales unlike its trout relatives. The tail, pectoral and anal fins are usually yellowish in color, but the pelvic fins usually have lengthwise stripes of black and pink.

The species used to be common in the Midwest, but became extinct in this century, though efforts are underway to restore historic populations. In the West, Lewis and Clark first discovered the fish during their expedition in 1805 and referred to the grayling as a "new kind of white or silvery trout." The last remaining stream-dwelling population in Montana is in the Big Hole River in the southwestern corner of the state.

Other Trout

Bull Trout

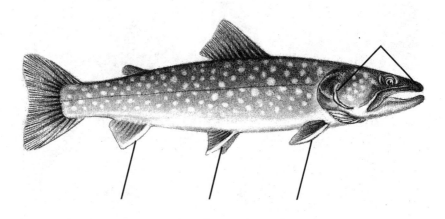

The bull trout's coloration ranges on the sides from silvery green to dark green with pinkish to whitish spots. Lower fins have white leading edges and its head is longer, broader and more flat than its cousin Dolly Varden.

Grayling are mature by three years, often as early as two and at this age they are about a foot long. The female lays several thousand eggs, but no redd is constructed. Most grayling live less than six years and a 2-pound fish is a trophy in the contiguous United States.

It is easy to see why the grayling is a member of the trout family. With the exception of the large scales, the species has the body shape of a trout and feeds on most of the same foods, including aquatic insects. Methods that take trout will catch grayling. Small is the word when fishing for grayling—⅛ ounce and smaller spinners and spoons, No. 14 or smaller hooks for bait and flies. Worms, maggots, nymphs, scuds, grasshoppers, beetles and crickets will take the fish in good numbers. Dry flies like the Adams, small caddis and mayfly imitations and black gnats will catch fish on every cast when they are schooling (which is the majority of the time) and feeding on the surface. Nymphs work well at other times.

Look for grayling in riffles, runs or resting in pools. In lakes, they can be anywhere but are often spotted aggressively feeding near downed trees and overhanging brush along shore. Inlets and outlets are another good place to find the fish, which put up a brief but lively fight when hooked.

Bull Trout

No one species of fish in the inland Northwest is less known, less appreciated, and at the same time, more representative of this rugged region than the bull trout. Bright orange spots on a silver and olive background (bright orange during spawning), and sizes of over 20 pounds, the bull trout makes an excellent gamefish. The average size of the species when caught in Montana is 8 pounds.

The fish was only recently differentiated from the Dolly Varden as a separate species. Bull trout are related to the brook trout and the two frequently hybridize when occupying the same waters. The main difference between the Dolly Varden and the bull trout is that the bull trout has a much flatter and wider head. The reason for this is that the bull trout has evolved to exist almost entirely on a diet of forage fish and other trout. The shape of the head makes ingestion of this food source much easier.

Bull trout spawn in the fall, moving up from lakes and rivers beginning in late spring and early summer as they migrate to their spawning tributaries. This distance can be over 50 miles which is an impressive journey for an inland freshwater fish. These char reach sexual maturity in the fourth or fifth year, and they pair up at the mouths of spawning streams before moving up to clean, well-oxygenated water to construct large redds. Silt from extensive logging in their native Columbia River Basin has greatly reduced their numbers throughout the Northwest, but some populations, notably those in northwest Montana, are showing increases in their numbers.

In addition to the bull trout's impressive size and exotic beauty during spawning, another attraction to fishing for the species is that this fish inhabits some of the wildest, least-developed and most-beautiful country in the world. Some of the best water lies in Glacier National Park and the Bob Marshall Wilderness, home to grizzlies, elk, goats, Rocky Mountain bighorn sheep and bald eagles.

Large spoons and plugs worked right through fast-water runs and deep pool holding areas often take the fish. Another prime

A 9-pound bull trout like this angler just caught would put a smile on any fisherman's face. However, bull trout are not a household name among most trout fishermen.

This bull trout weighed 14 pounds when netted. While that is big, bulls have been known to weigh as much as 20 pounds. They're found in the Northwest's pure, wilderness waters.

spot is large logjams where very big trout hold. Snorkling for these fish during fisheries department survey counts can be a frightening experience, especially for those observers who come face-to-face with a 15-pound fish tucked away in a jumble of tree limbs. As many as several dozen casts with small spoons or large streamers may be required to provoke a strike from the fish during spawning time. Among experienced fly fishers for bull trout, saltwater patterns such as bendbacks are gaining increasing acceptance.

In lakes, fishing large red-and-white or silver or brass spoons off of points and drop-offs is the most productive method. In still water the fish are cruisers, working the shoreline looking for smaller fish. The best times to fish are early in the morning or after sunset. Bull trout truly do not like high-intensity light.

Other Trout

Once the light level drops in the evening, they become active.

Ten-pound test line and stout tippets are needed when fishing for bull trout. The fish do not jump. Rather, when hooked, they turn and steadily run downstream pulling line off your reel. A large one cannot be checked, so an angler often must follow a bull trout downriver until it is exhausted.

Dolly Varden

Dolly Varden take their name from Charles Dickens' character, Miss Dolly Varden, of the book *Baranby Rudge*. Miss Varden was always wearing dresses with pink spots and the fish is marked with pink to orange spots along its silvery green flanks and back. At least this is the common explanation but a careful reading of the book turns up only the mention of the woman wearing a cherry-colored dress, so who really knows the origin of this colorful name?

Until recently this western char was considered to be the same fish as the bull trout, but the Dolly's narrower head and propensity toward anadromous behavior, along with several morphological (form and structure) differences, convinced biologists that the two were separate species. In its sea-run form, it is silvery, while in small, mountain headwater streams the spotting may lean toward crimson and the body color dark green. The fins have the distinctive white tipping found on most chars. Weights average around 5 pounds and the species runs generally smaller than the bull trout.

Dolly Varden are found from northern California up the Pacific Coast to Alaska and around the northern Pacific Rim from Japan to Korea and in some Siberian waters. The fish is slow-growing, as is the bull trout, but has a life span approaching 20 years in fortuitous specimens.

The char are voracious feeders on salmon eggs which does little for their popularity among West Coast salmon fishers. The trout also take aquatic insects in much greater numbers than bull trout, so while methods that catch bulls will catch Dolly Varden, the baitfisher that uses salmon eggs drift fishing will usually score heavily. The day-glo egg patterns common among Alaska fly fishers also work as do some large dry flies on occasion. Big is beautiful and there really is no such thing as "matching the hatch" with Dollys.

One last place to look for the fish is in shallow runs just below deep pools. This water is normally full of oxygen and delivers a steady supply of food. The species is at home here.

Apache Trout

The Apache trout is also known as the Arizona trout and now provides a trophy fishery on a limited permit basis in a few streams and lakes on the Fort Apache Indian Reservation in the White Mountains of Arizona. The fish was saved, at least temporarily, from extinction by an artificial propagation program using pure-strain eggs from the wild population. The Arizona Game & Fish Department has maintained this program with good results.

The fish resemble the cutthroat in most respects with some similarities to the rainbow, mainly in the absence of hyoid teeth. The waters of the Apache are scattered over wild plateau and mountain country between the Salt and Black rivers and the Mogollon Rim.

In lakes, the fish will exceed a pound in weight, in streams 12 inches is large. The Apache's body is dominated by yellow along the back, becoming lighter along the sides and belly. Black spots are evenly distributed along the chunky body above the lateral line. The lower fins are tipped in white. The most unusual feature of the Apache is the black bar across the eye.

For the angler, dry flies such as a No. 12 Adams work as well as anything when tempting this species.

Gila Trout

This species was first described in 1950. Prior to this time the Gila trout was considered a cutthroat. The range of this fish is restricted to the Gila River in New Mexico and Arizona along with Ord Creek, and Diamond, McKenna and Spruce creeks in New Mexico. Stocking in recent years has expanded this range somewhat.

The Gila is dark olive on the back giving way to golden yellow on its belly. Small black spots mark the length of the body and tail. The fish is of minor angling value and protected by regulations. It hybridizes easily with other trout and feeds primarily on the nymphal forms of caddis flies, mayflies and midges. An 8-inch Gila trout is about average.

When you're looking for trout, you need look no farther than a stretch of water like this. To a trout fisherman it has the "look and feel" of water that will yield Dolly Vardens and other trout.

Mexican Golden Trout

Chrystogaster, the Latin species name for this fish, is derived from the Greek meaning "golden belly," the most discernible characteristic of this fish. The golden color is also present along the lower jaw. The fish inhabits small streams of a 1,500-square-mile area in the Fuerte, Sinola and Culiacan rivers systems of southwestern Chihauhua and northwestern Durango in Mexico.

The native waters of the Mexican golden are above 8,000 feet in extremely rugged, isolated, almost inaccessible terrain. Few have fished for the species, but report that the trout takes dry flies and reaches 12 inches maximum. Not much else is known about the fish from an angling standpoint.

Sunapee Trout

The Sunapee is considered a landlocked population of arctic char and is closely related to the blueback and Marston trout. The fish's namesake water is Sunapee Lake in New Hampshire. Other populations are known to exist in Vermont and Maine.

The fish resembles a less-colorful brook trout and 12 inches is a big Sunapee. In the summer the trout holds in water up to 100 feet deep at temperatures of about 50 degrees. It spawns in late fall. The fish hybridizes with both lake and brook trout, and the only pure strain of Sunapee is thought to exist in Floods Pond, Maine.

Handlining or deep trolling with smelt bait produces the few fish that anglers manage to take each season, and these could very well be hybrids.

Finding Trout

9

Rivers And Streams

There is a reason that trout are found in so many different types of water in so many parts of North America. They have evolved into creatures that can eat an astounding variety of food. These sources of nutrients, chiefly protein, come in hundreds of different forms from aquatic insects to terrestrials to minnows and other forage fish to crustaceans to worms, grubs, maggots and spawn. Larger trout will and do eat frogs, mice and other small rodents. This eclectic diet also includes specimens such as butterflies, moths, algae and even sewage.

Huge trout are taken every year throughout the country by anglers fishing below municipal waste treatment plant discharge areas. If the creature provides calories, is found in or near the water and is small enough to swallow, or at least take a bite out of, at one time or another it has been eaten by a trout. The selection is almost endless and some of the creatures trout consume have not even been discovered yet or given names by the scientific community.

This section will be broken down into chapters dealing with rivers and streams; lakes, reservoirs and ponds; spring creeks; and the Great Lakes. Behavior, life cycle and optimum locations will be discussed and examined. Since many trout food sources are normally found in rivers and streams, they will initially be discussed in some depth. Other food sources that are only associated with a given type of water will be discussed in

An effective way to cover miles and miles of good holding water on a trout stream is using a drift boat. You can pull over and fish choice locations thoroughly as this angler did in taking a rainbow.

Rivers And Streams

detail in the appropriate chapter. Baits such as salmon eggs, corn, maggots, marshmallows and nightcrawlers will be dealt with in the section on tackle dealing with bait.

The Advantage Of Moving Water

Moving water offers trout a greater variety of food sources than any other environment, and, in most cases, all the fish has to do is just wait for something to eat to come drifting right past its holding area.

This abundance of food, coupled with usually cool, well-oxygenated water and adequate cover, results in truly astounding sizes of trout in some very small streams. Every year stories appear in local newspapers describing how some angler caught a 6- or 7-pound trout in the local creek that was, at most, 4 feet wide. As long as there is a sheltered pocket for the fish to hide in with proper water conditions, trout will do just fine. Most anglers spent sizable portions of their early lives exploring a neighborhood creek or even a nearby drainage ditch. Beetles, mayflies, frogs and hundreds of tiny minnows lived there in profusion and, once again, as long as the water conditions were okay, so did trout.

Pools, riffles and runs, banks and fixed objects in the current all provide ideal places for trout to quietly hide and wait for a convenient meal to appear. Also, all four of these environments frequently hold at least marginal populations of the major "food groups."

A stream is so rich in food that enticing a trout into taking an angler's offering sometimes borders on impossible and an individual's efforts to attract the fish's attentions requires great forethought and cunning. Turning a trout's eye and then actually convincing it on some wild level of consciousness to ingest what is being drifted, swum or dropped in its holding area takes on epic proportions of high art—a human successfully imitating nature.

Many times our efforts are unsuccessful, particularly when there are a variety of food sources on or in the water and the trout have keyed to only one of them. The classic example of this is when a fly fisher makes cast after perfect cast over a rising trout with a pattern that appears to exactly match the insect hatch; yet, these diligent efforts go unrewarded and extreme

The calm water adjacent to the fast, rippling water of the outside bend (lower right) on this stream is a good spot to pick up fish by drifting bait, spinners or nymphs along the bottom.

frustration sets in. Situations like this are complex, and normally there are several species of insects hatching or about to hatch at once—or the fish may be focusing on just one phase of a specific insect, like the stone fly nymph which may be struggling to the surface.

True, there are those days when you could "throw your car keys in the water and catch fish." However, anglers who experience consistent success, not just in hooking small fish, are those that know where the best holding areas are, what food sources are present and spend time before beginning to fish observing the water for signs of rising fish, hatching insects, darting minnows—anything that will help narrow odds that are heavily stacked in favor of the trout.

Understanding the four basic types of habitat in a stream,

including the various food sources likely to be found in each one, will push an angler a good distance along the learning curve. From this point on, the angler builds on past experiences and is not perplexed (or at least hopefully not for long) or intimidated by situations that feature combinations of environments such as an undercut bank along a riffle or run, or a fixed object within a pool. These situations are all variations of the universal theme.

Another problem is found when an angler encounters a large river, like those found in the West. Where do you begin to fish? There is so much water. Once you understand the basics, finding fish is easier. Rivers are basically upscale versions of small streams. The dynamics and related principles present in the lesser water, hold true for big, brawling flows.

Pools Are Lake-Stream Combinations

Driving along a road that parallels a river or stream or hiking up over a rise and spotting a wild creek, an angler's excitement is triggered by a pool of deep, clear, turquoise water. A swift run or waterfall defines the head of this miniature pond and often a smooth glide or another cascade marks the downstream boundary. "There just have to be fish in here," is his first thought. And there usually are, but no other type of habitat is so consistently misunderstood or improperly fished, even by skilled trout fishers.

This water looks too "trouty" to him to display patience and to take the time to analyze and plan his approach. He shakily rigs up his rods and plunges headlong into the water eager to make that first cast and catch that huge trout that he knows has been waiting all day for his "skillful" attention. Unfortunately, these wild actions have probably created a trout stampede down to the next pool or even the next one after that. Even the boys from Rawhide could not have checked this wild ride. He has messed up—big time—and made a key tactical error. If the clarity of the pool allows an angler to look deep down inside it, think what the view must be for the trout who live in it 24 hours a day all year, sometimes for a decade.

The Big Three Insects Of Pool Habitats

At any given time of the season there is apt to be insect

The Mayfly Life Cycle

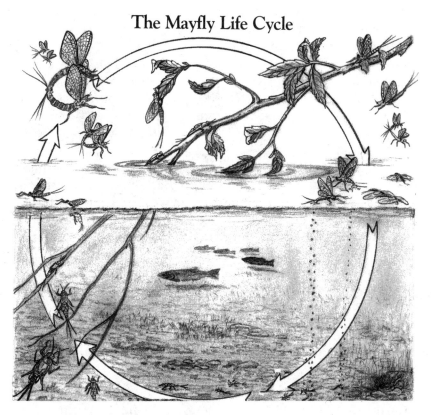

Understanding the mayfly life cycle can be important in taking trout. From the time that the nymphs emerge from the streambed until the adult takes off from the water, an angler will do well if he duplicates the life-cycle stages through selection and presentation of artificials.

activity around pools, and often this will be in the form of mayflies. Over 500 species of mayflies (Family Ephemeroptera) have been identified in North America and new ones are turned up every year. Varying in size from ⅛ inch to 1½ inches, mayflies are identified by three (or sometimes two) narrow tails, a large front pair of wings and small hind pair, visibly veined and folded at rest in a distinctive vertical position. The winged stages of the species have atrophied digestive tracts and are incapable of feeding. No other food source for trout receives as much attention from anglers (and perhaps the trout themselves) as the mayfly. The species has been studied for centuries. Trout feed on nymphs, duns (the hatching, emerging form) and spinners (the mating and egg-laying forms) wherever they are present, which is wherever there is water.

Some of the more important species are the Hendrickson, green Drake, olive dun, brown Drake, dark Cahill, gray fox and burrowing mayfly (mistakenly referred to as a Michigan caddis).

Found in perhaps even greater abundance than mayflies are caddis flies, with nearly 1,000 species identified on this continent. Also abundant in almost any type of water, the caddis fly can be anywhere from ⅛ inch to over 2 inches in overall length.

The caddis fly larvae make protective cases out of small gravels, sticks and almost anything else usable on the stream bottom. The species experiences a similar life cycle as that of the mayfly. Adults have tent-like wings folded across their backs when resting and resemble tiny helicopters during flight. Some important species for the angler are the White Miller, Autumn Phantom and American Sedge. This family ranks a very close second to mayflies when talking about importance as a food source for trout.

Last and largest among the "Big Three" of aquatic insects on the trout dietary hit parade is the stone fly and over 400 species of this family have been identified in the U.S. and Canada. While some species are only ⅛ inch long, many are over 2 inches with 4-inch wing spans. Most of the insects are gray or brown, some are yellow and a few green and quite similar to caddis in form, but always with two tails. The nymphs, which prefer faster water than the other two families and must have absolutely pure water, crawl out of the water onto rocks, bushes and tree trunks to shed their skins and dry their wings. This usually occurs during the night or early morning, but, be prepared for like the other emerging aquatic insects, it can occur at any time of the day.

Important species of stone fly include the yellow Sally, willow and Western salmonfly which hatch in such profusion that the sky is literally obscured by the whirring insects during May and June. This is an angling event of epic proportions in the Rocky Mountains.

There is a very good chance that one or more species of all three of these families will be found in a specific pool environment. They can be found anywhere, including buried in the submerged sand and gravels, crawling on the sides and undersides of rocks and boulders, on weed seams or moving

Caddis-fly nymphs will often build protective cases from small gravels found on the bottom of the stream. Trout will eat these, stones and all.

along sticks and logs. Before you approach the water to fish, examine the surface of the stream and the air directly above it to see if any insect activity is taking place. If nothing is happening, approach and examine the streambed downstream (from a pool you consider to be prime) to determine if any nymphs are present (and if this is a trout stream, they will be).

Lesser Lights Of The Insect World

There are other insect sources common to streams and rivers, but of lesser importance.

Dragonflies and damselflies are far more common in lakes but are a minor food source in moving water. The nymphs of both are often olive green shading to black. Winged versions can range from bright blue to black. These creatures of the insect world and trout streams prefer slack or very slow-moving water.

Dobsonflies include the larval stage known as hellgrammite by many anglers. The mature larvae may exceed 3 inches in length. The winged adult is, at best, a minor food source. Look for these in slow water also.

While true flies (Diptera) number over 15,000 species, only a few play any role in a trout's diet as do craneflies that have extremely productive hatches on some rivers such as the Beaverhead in Montana where these large mosquito-like insects draw big browns and rainbows to the surface in a feeding frenzy during late summer. They like moving water and are easy to spot as they lumber above the river's surface.

Finally, nonbiting midges seldom exceed ¾ inch but are an important trout food source. They resemble mosquitoes and emerge in large swarms. The larvae are known by some as "blood worms."

Blackflies, in larval forms that crawl along the upstream faces of rocks and boulders in swiftly flowing streams, are an important food for young trout.

Remember, all of these species will be found at one time or another throughout the pool habitat, but the choice locations are those that include the basics of shelter, oxygenated water and current to deliver the food to the waiting fish (and in similar fashion to the often voracious insects). Fish the quickening currents at the downstream side of the pool, below entering riffles, runs and falls, and along the edges of any current seams visible by shifting, flickering variations in the otherwise smooth surface of the pool.

Currents Often Hold Forage Fish

The bright, bubbling flow of water as it bounces and dances in riffles off a variegated streambed of coarse gravels, rocks and even small boulders is considered to have fewer fish than pools. The current is often too fast for trout, even for the rainbow, that are often associated with this river feature. The same is believed to hold true for deep, hard-charging runs that surge darkly downstream.

To some extent these perceptions of swift current have a good deal of truth, but at certain times and in the right locations they can be spots of superb angling action. Both areas

Trout Locations In Beaver Ponds

Old streambeds (F) are a prime location for trout in beaver ponds. Other spots to check are around debris (A), ridge lines (B), steep holes (C), divided current (D), areas with shade and overhead cover (E), an undercut bank (G), weedbeds (H), submerged cover (I) and the pond's inlet (J).

provide well-oxygenated, cool, frequently cold, water in abundance. Because of the broken surface of these stretches, trout feel safe, if only for brief feeding forays. The obstructions that make up the beds of these regions offer depressions sufficient to harbor trout of surprising size, often in good numbers. An added bonus is that forage fish often thrive here, as do certain types of insects. Forage fish are energy-efficient meals for trout. A minimum amount of energy is expended to attain a large piece of protein. Where there are forage fish there are trout.

Prominent among these small baitfish is the sculpin clan—a family that thrives in riffles and runs, often burrowing under the smaller gravels found behind rocks and boulders, and even digging under small rocks. Trout love these baitfish that have names like mottled, slimy, torrent, shorthead and spoonhead. Sculpin are commonly found in sizes of between 2 and 6 inches. They will never win a beauty contest with their wide heads, large mouths and quickly-tapering bodies. Their most distinctive feature is the big, billowing pectoral fins that enable the species to move around in the somewhat calm bottom currents. Often, these calm bottom zones are no more than an inch in depth, explaining the evolution of the flattened body shape.

Where sculpin and trout populations are high, it is not uncommon to find the forage fish drifting lifelessly near shore with large bites taken out of their bodies—fatal wounds from the predations of hefty trout. They provide food year-round. Big browns will often come up at night off shelves they've rested on during the day just below the riffles and runs and attack the sculpins. Fishing at these times is exciting, and an angler can often hear a big trout slicing through the water or even see the wake of a brown as it hunts down sculpin.

The same is true for the darter and dace families. The two prefer rapid current and cold water, seldom exceed 4 inches in length and look remarkably like sculpins. There are approximately 85 species of sculpin, and there are over 95 darters with fancy names like fountain, harlequin, orangethroat and fantail. Dace are not as prolific but have names like blacknose, longnose and speckled. When these species are present locally, they are a prime trout food source.

Insects Also Important In Riffles And Runs

Of the big three aquatic insects, stone flies are the most important in riffles and runs because of their preference for fast-flowing water. Hatching throughout the year in this environment, the May-June emergence of the salmonfly in the West is the classic riffle/run insect activity. Lesser numbers of caddis and mayfly nymphs will also be found in this habitat.

While trout will feed on the random offerings delivered from the swift current, they are waiting primarily for the food sources just mentioned. One advantage to riffles, often overlooked by anglers who figure the frequently shallow water is devoid of fish, is large trout will move into these areas even on a bright day with the sun blazing directly overhead. They know there is food there, and they also know that they are just a short

Natural And Man-Made Structure In Trout Streams

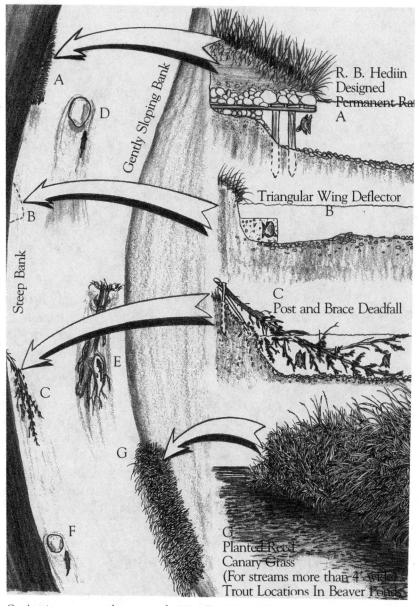

R. B. Hediin
Designed
Permanent Rock
A

Triangular Wing Deflector
B

C
Post and Brace Deadfall

Gently Sloping Bank

Steep Bank

A
D
B
C
E
G
F

G
Planted Reed
Canary Grass
(For streams more than 4' wide)
Trout Locations In Beaver Ponds

Overhanging structure either man-made (A), (B), (C), (G) or natural (D), (E), shorelines. Grasshoppers, beetles, ants, etc. often fall in a trout's feeding and sweep food right into their quiet holding areas. The same is true of other obstructions such as submerged or buried logs (E). Man-made or natural current deflectors (B) where permitted channel food and oxygen-rich water through certain areas. Trout hold in quieter areas on the edges of these swift flows.

distance from safety even if a predator can spot them in the broken current. When other portions of a river or stream shut down during the heat and brightness of midday, riffles and runs can provide top-notch angling.

Freestone Streams: Pocket Pools

Freestone streams, those creeks and rushing torrents that pour out of the likes of the Smoky Mountains, Adirondacks, Rockies and countless other ranges, do not fit into any specific category. Because the streams drop at such a steep gradient, trout are forced to take up residence in any miniature pool or pocket of water that will hold them. These little oases of tranquility are often no more than a foot in diameter, but are just big and deep enough to shelter a trout. These fish cannot afford to be selective because food rushes by at such a rapid clip. Anything that vaguely resembles a recognizable food source is snatched and just as quickly expelled if the fish's senses indicate something undesirable or suspicious. Any spot that even vaguely resembles a pool on a freestone stream can hold a trout and perhaps some caddis or stone fly nymphs. These tumbling, rocky streams are a harsh environment despite their aesthetically pleasing appearance to the angler.

Banks Mean Terrestrials

Trout, being creatures of stealth and secrecy, love anything they can hide under or anyplace they can disappear. Tangled logjams, piles of rocks and especially brushy, undercut banks create perfect cover. Because an undercut means that a river's current has been at work driving water against the earth and rock, it indicates that a regular flow of food is washed through the area. Shelter and food—what more could any big-time trout want in life?

Add to the equation the fact that crickets, ants, beetles, bees, grasshoppers and, yes, even butterflies often miscalculate and land on a stream's surface film and you have a safe, readily available source of protein for trout, particularly browns, to allow them to grow fat and happy.

One food item you will not find with any degree of frequency here are forage fish. Undercut banks have some areas of shelter and moderate current, but the best places are taken by

Small Stream Pocket-Water Areas

Overhead view of small stream sections of pocket water.

In working small-stream pocket-water areas, the angler should stay downstream and work bank-eddy pockets (A), pockets above and below exposed mid-stream boulders (B), undercut bank pockets (C), drop-off pockets below riffle (D) and riffle pockets (E) front to back to avoid spooking fish.

big fish. The remainder of the water in an undercut is often a swift rush of force that is too much for the little fish to hold.

Most of the terrestrial insects trout are accustomed to finding in undercuts do not become active until well after the sun has climbed up in the sky and warmed the air. Early in the morning grasshoppers are easy pickings for the baitfisher. Their metabolisms are still sluggish from the cool of the past night, but as soon as they heat up from the sun, you will find them leaping and soaring everywhere in the grass and through the bushes. The same holds true for other insects. Many of them make mistakes and plop in the water. Trout holding along banks start to key in on this food source about midmorning and throughout the day. As soon as the weather warms and the insects become active, the trout start feeding on them. After the first hard frost of the year, this source of easy food is pretty well finished for the season.

Crafty old fish have even been known to rattle branches and brush overhanging leaves with their noses in order to dislodge ants and other insects into their feeding lanes. Other choice locations include log or tree-limb sweepers lying across the current from the bank, piles of rocks or boulders along or near shore, fences crossing streams and basically any obstruction extended out into the water from shore. Anything that slows the current and provides shelter.

Because banks provide shaded shelter, trout lose their midday bright-light wariness and will feed consistently throughout the daylight hours when other areas of a river are commonly devoid of action.

Late in the summer, on nutrient-rich streams where roots are exposed or branches from overhanging bushes extend into the current enough to disrupt and slow down the speed of the moving water, algae will begin to bloom and eventually form large mats that run down along and out from the bank. These mats are filled with insects of all types, and really large trout will often rest under these spots and hit anything swept into, under or alongside of the natural carpets.

Scuds, which resemble shrimp but are actually amphipods, are commonly associated with a lake environment, but will often be found in quiet areas of weed or algae growth alongside banks and similar areas, and to a much lesser extent in pools. They are a significant food source for trout, especially in Western rivers. Often green or olive in color, scuds range in size from ¼- to ¾-inch long and provide year-round forage.

Come fall when the browns are on their spawning runs, you will find fish along rocky or gravel-covered stretches of bank in water that is so shallow you can see their backs and dorsal fins shining in the golden fall light and crisp air. They move into these areas to feed on any late-season terrestrials or on any small minnows darting around, and also to rest during their tiresome upstream migrations.

While the heads and tails of pools and narrow stretches of riffles and runs remain generally ice-free during most of winter, banks are normally frozen solid or piled high with an accumulation of ice delivered by the current. Banks are

Large Stream Pocket-Water Areas

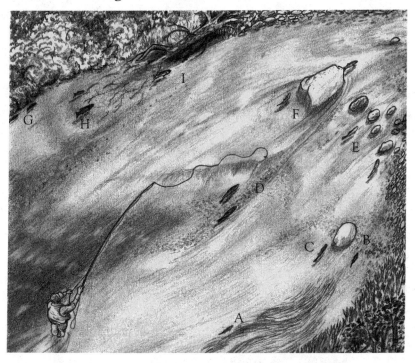

This overhead view of large-stream, pocket-water areas shows the number of areas that need to be worked. Work lures, bait and flies along the sides, front and back of moss beds (A), water breaking over gravel bar (B), a boulder in slower water (C), bedrock faults (D), fast-riffle rubble (E), surface boulder (F), bank edges with cover (G), logs or fallen trees (H) and deadfalls (I).

three-season water for the trout fisherman.

Picking The Pockets Of Fixed Objects

Water in front of, swirling around and past, and lying behind fixed objects in the current holds trout. Perhaps the fish are not as large as those found in pools or along banks (size of habitat really does equate to size of fish), but there will always be trout among boulders in the middle of streams, along downed trees lying parallel to the flow—within anything that blocks or changes the course of a river.

Fishing this water is called "picking pockets" by some skilled anglers because the water that holds fish is small—a small pocket in the fabric of a big river.

Many anglers are unaware of the good pocket water lying in

front of a midstream obstruction. Water piles up against something like a boulder and gouges out a substantial depression, creating a perfect, quiet, sheltered place for trout to hide. The trout can streak up from this location and snatch any passing food source like insects or minnows tumbling in the current. Figuring the force of the water would pin a trout against a rock, anglers often pass up this water, even on streams that experience heavy fishing pressure elsewhere.

To a lesser extent, this holds true alongside obstructions where similar but smaller zones exist. Trout waiting behind rocks also rush into these zones to grab a quick bite.

The feeding in these two spots is normally along the bottom where the current is at its weakest. Near the surface, the water is running so strongly that even strong swimmers like rainbows have difficulty maneuvering.

Another prime mid-current pocket lies behind midstream objects. A river's current swirls and forms eddies back there. In the center, the water is calm like the eye of a hurricane and fish hold steady in wait for food that spins into the liquid storm. Nymphs crawl along the sandy and gravelled streambeds in these areas and trout casually pick them off. Often, you will find trout facing what would appear to be downstream but is in reality upstream because of the swirling and hence reversing nature of the current. This, too, is water that either is passed by or incorrectly fished by most anglers.

The main sources of food found in the area of fixed objects are aquatic insects and whatever is washed downstream. Terrestrials rarely stray this far from the bank and minnows are uncommon. Crossing the harsh main-stem currents is usually an impossibility for small fish.

At times of low water, during the height of summer, and into autumn before seasonal rains replenish streamflows, midstream obstructions often provide pool-like or spring-like habitat (a major difference here being that springs normally contain high levels of carbon dioxide and little oxygen) for trout as a result of the fairly deep depressions dug in the streambed during periods of higher flow. Cool, sheltered water can still be found in these locations. During winter, this water is often open because of the speed of the current which must increase to pass around these objects. Trout often move to the larger depressions in the streambed for the winter.

Rivers And Streams Offer A Bit Of Everything

When approaching rivers and streams, you must be prepared for a variety of conditions ranging from fast, rushing water to deep pools that often resemble small lakes or ponds to deep, undercut banks that are basically submerged caves holding the big trout you're searching.

These types of water offer a variety of habitats and a multitude of food sources. Unlike lakes that remain relatively stable over the years, rivers change from year to year and sometimes a familiar run or pool will have changed drastically or disappeared altogether in the course of a week.

Just when an angler figures he knows where to find a trout's food sources and the trout themselves, the entire picture changes and a new environment and set of problems present themselves. As long as the basics associated with each type of water are taken into account, the search should be relatively brief in duration and productive in nature.

=========10=========

Lakes And Reservoirs

Part of every veteran trout fisher's memory package includes the mental picture of a lake at sunset, its surface mirror-smooth, gun-metal gray in color. Towering dark pines grow down to the shore. Perhaps a ridge of rugged, snowcapped mountains carves its way across the horizon. The sound of running water resounds through the forest. Trout are dimpling the water by the dozens—no, make that by the hundreds as they delicately sip emerging caddis before the flies lift off from the lake into the air.

Every cast (in memory factual accuracy is not of paramount interest) takes a fish that immediately leaps, tailwalks and splashes its way 100 feet toward the far shore. After several minutes, the glowing rainbow-cutthroat-brook trout comes grudgingly to net admired by the awed angler who, now feeling such kindred respect and admiration for the fish, gently revives it in the calm water before releasing the creature to swim back into the silent depths.

There are not many anglers around who do not, or would not, cherish such an experience, and outings like this one are not uncommon. But then, neither are those days where the same lake looks pretty much mirror-smooth again and the same old sun is setting over that mountain ridge—with one major difference. There are no fish to be seen or for that matter found. After 10,000 casts, the angler is convinced there are not any fish, and probably never were, and he could care less if there

Working lily pads and downed logs on lakes will produce trout. A float tube is a good way to fish this water thoroughly and efficiently.

Lakes And Reservoirs

was ever going to be trout in these parts in the future because he's had enough of this nonsense and is never going to fish again. Ever.

Sound familiar? If you fish lakes or reservoirs to any extent, days like the latter are not unfamiliar. Nothing is so frustrating as working a piece of still water hard for hours knowing that there are good numbers of big fish swimming there—somewhere. Lake fishing can make an angler feel foolish, inept, depressed and angry simultaneously. And while there is no guaranteed system for finding (the catching comes later) trout on every outing, there are a number of things to look for and to be aware of that definitely can shift the odds in your direction.

Major Lake Types And Zones

The three major types of lakes that concern the trout fisher are the oligotrophic (or scant nourishment), eutrophic (well-nourished) and impoundments (or reservoirs).

Oligotrophic lakes are infants in the aging process and are usually deep and clear with few nutrients. Any fish or plants living here will be small, unless they happen to be very old. Eventually, these lakes will evolve into eutrophic lakes as their tributaries deliver nutrients and sediment to them. This may take thousands of years.

Eutrophic lakes are shallower and have much greater aquatic plant growth. As a result, they commonly have many more and larger trout.

There are basically four major zones to most lakes—littoral, limnetic, profundal, and inlets and outlets. Shorelines are either littoral, limnetic, a combination of the two, or influenced by inlets and outlets. Roughly speaking, the three scientific terms refer to the surface, the middle layer and the bottom of a lake or reservoir. Each has a different chemical composition which is extremely important when finding trout is an issue.

The littoral zone is the region where rooted plants grow. In shallow bodies of water this can include the entire lake. The region is most commonly associated with shorelines but can also include shoals. Lakes with abrupt drop-offs, or turbid water have limited littoral zones. Many reservoirs on the high plains

Fishing points, especially those with reed beds, tree stumps or other structure will take trout. Work the edges first and then work into the interior of the structure.

or in the desert basins of the West are subject to fierce winds that blow days at a time, creating strong wave action that scours the shoreline areas clear of any silt or mud that is needed to hold rooted plants in place. Despite this lack of growth, the area is still considered a littoral zone because light can still penetrate to the very bottom.

Impoundments are artificial structures and have numerous variables such as drawdowns from dams for irrigation or power generating purposes. Because of this, the littoral zone often varies widely with the fluctuation in water levels making the location of trout as much a matter of luck at times as observation and experience. Reservoirs are often shallower than natural lakes and tend to suffer more often from warming, siltation and turbidity.

In deeper lakes where light cannot reach the bottom but does exert some influence on the deeper middle layers of water permitting the growth of plants including algae, the region is referred to as the limnetic zone.

The third area is the profundal zone, a region that receives little if any light. Any creatures that live here exist on food and organic debris that sift down from above.

Inlets and outlets tend to combine the characteristics of both lakes and streams into one specific area. If an angler has never been to a specific lake, one of his best bets is to work these areas. Rivers and streams entering a lake bring much-needed nutrients and add oxygen to the system. Outlets tend to carry away debris and silt that eventually clog and fill up a lake. Aquatic insects, minnows and assorted other creatures such as frogs, on rare occasions crayfish (which prefer waters that are too warm for trout) and other small crustaceans congregate here. Outlets also wash down a steady stream of food that also includes terrestrials along with the above snack mix. Because of this gathering of food sources, trout show up in healthy numbers. This happens at all times of the year and usually throughout the day, regardless of weather conditions.

Trout Surface For Obvious Reasons

The surface, or littoral zone, has the greatest concentration of food sources for trout and, as a result, more trout than any other lake zone.

Because the surface of a lake is the zone most directly affected by the elements, it is normally the area with the highest concentration of dissolved gases. Oxygen and carbon dioxide are the two most important of these. Trout need at least 10 parts per million of oxygen to survive and this compound enters a lake through the mix of the atmosphere with the water from wave action, especially along broken shorelines and rocky points, explaining why these locations often contain fish. The other major influx of oxygen occurs when photosynthesis occurs in aquatic plants. Obviously, for this process to take place, carbon dioxide is necessary.

Carbon dioxide enters a lake through a variety of means including being dissolved in rainwater or in groundwater or springs, plant and animal respiration in the water and the decomposition of organic matter.

While none of this is as exciting as actually fighting a 5-pound rainbow racing across the lake's surface, the information is the key to understanding and finding food sources and then the trout. For example, it takes several hundred pounds of algae to produce sufficient nutrients to, in turn, produce sufficient aquatic insect growth to create 1 pound of trout. Without oxygen and carbon dioxide, little if any of this growth can occur. And so it goes.

With the exception of those species of forage fish and aquatic insects that have evolved exclusively toward a freshwater environment, everything a trout eats in a river can also be found in a lake or reservoir. In the West, in many reservoirs, populations of scuds are so dense that an angler's waders will be covered with the animals when he exits the water. Trout feast on these crustaceans and grow to tremendous size quickly, in some waters as much as 1 inch per month for the first two years. These fish are fat and wide and also extremely selective, and most often are difficult to fool. There are over 50 species of scuds, most of them located in the western U.S. They feed on almost anything and are found swimming and darting about among concentrations of aquatic vegetation. Trout feed on these tiny animals throughout the day and year.

Dragonflies And Damselflies Important Food

Another major source of food that is much more important in lakes than in rivers are damselflies and dragonflies. There are well over 400 species in this insect family, most living in still water. They may be anywhere from 1 to 5 inches long. Dragonfly nymphs are much more rounded and bulky than damselfly nymphs with their elongated, slender shape. Adult dragonflies are normally larger than damselflies and dragonflies also have larger wings that frequently have banded patterns on them. Body colors of adult dragonflies may be just about any shade. Damselflies most often portray a bright, almost neon blue body color.

Both creatures can maneuver extremely well in flight, flitting and darting above the lake surface feeding on other insects including mosquitoes. Dragonflies will establish regular flight patterns that extend for several miles, unlike damselflies

Finding Trout In Lakes

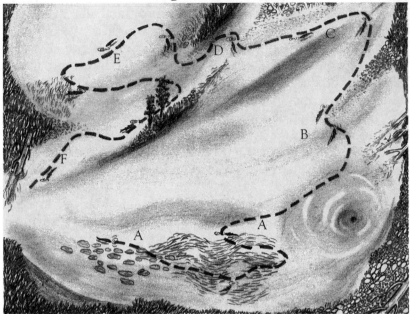

Trout often have travel routes (dotted line) to and from the best foraging areas. Moss or weedbeds (A) hold large numbers of aquatic insects in nymphal form as well as providing hiding areas for minnows and forage areas for scuds—all classic trout foods. Food blows in along rocky points (B). Inlets (C) and mouths of feeder streams (D) are natural food conveyors for trout. Flats (E) provide good vantage points for trout to feed on passing food sources. Islands (E) or other obstructions allow trout to safely lie and wait for passing minnows or insects, as do rocky, offshore spots. (F).

which are localized fliers with short range.

Concentrations of both dragonfly and damselfly nymphs and winged adults can be found around weedbeds and clusters of lily pads where the nymphs are often seen crawling from the water, before shedding their skins and drying their wings prior to first flight. Trout will congregate in these areas. On windy days, the bodies of the spent insects concentrate along wind slicks, against plants and along shorelines and points. Trout cruise these areas, gulping large quantities of the species. This is true in spades, especially during the heat of day from late spring on through early fall.

Large Trout Dine On Baitfish In Lakes

In Upper Midwestern and Western lakes and reservoirs in

particular, trout often exceed 10 pounds and as a result, other fish become an important part of their diet. This includes their own kind. In a body of water with a known population of monster trout, areas such as inlets and outlets, narrow channels and shallow, weedy spots attract big trout which cruise in search of an easy meal. This activity is strongest at dusk and on into the evening, as well as in early morning.

Structure Important In Shallows, Too

Even (or perhaps especially) in shallow-water areas, bottom structure is important. Where beds of aquatic plants are not present, those bottoms that are uneven jumbles of rocks, boulders and debris will always have more food, and trout, than smooth, sandy or slick, hard-rock shelves. Obviously, the convoluted terrain offers infinitely more places for a minnow, small trout or nymph to hide and feed. Muddy or silted-in bottoms often have good populations of minnows and insects. Unfortunately, in most cases, the fact that they are full of muck is a good indication that there is not adequate current to satisfy the diverse requirements of the trout. Obviously, a layer of silt is necessary for plants to take root in, but when the treacherous stuff starts rising higher than your shins, more often than not, the area is unproductive from a trout standpoint. A big exception to this is when small springs bubble up through the silt, spreading cool, clear water. Large fish often gather around these areas early in the morning and at dusk searching for forage. Because of the high degree of exposure trout are subjected to in this shallow, open water, daylight hours are often fishless periods. (Another classic exception is a spring creek which will be discussed in the next chapter).

The surface or littoral zones of lakes are always places of fertility, even during turnover when temperature zones reverse themselves. In the summer, the warmer water is at the surface. In the winter, the warmer water is at the bottom of a lake. Most of an angler's trout fishing (with lake trout being a notable exception) will occur in this zone.

Mid-Depths Are Hot At Times

While the middle portions of a lake rarely contain the abundance and variety of food sources that the surface zone does, these areas can be the best places to fish at times. Unfortunately, this widely variable region is by far the most difficult to fish. The best depths may be located anywhere from a few yards to many feet deep, depending upon water clarity, which dictates the depth to which sunlight can penetrate in sufficient intensity to spark plant growth.

This zone can include drop-offs right next to shore or out at the edge of sandy beaches or dense growths of weeds. Trout will hold down below these shallow areas throughout the day and come up to feed on the insects, scuds and minnows and smaller trout that swim in the shallower water. Any drop-off near aquatic plant growth found in any lake is likely to hold suspended fish, sometimes not far below the surface.

Lake trout are often caught at depths well over 150 feet one week and then at 40 or 50 feet the next. All of this is dependent upon water temperature, weather conditions and time of day and year—factors that dictate the behavior of both trout and their food sources. Even if an individual knows a lake like the back of his hand, he is going to need some help on most days (or nights when fishing is often most productive, especially on big lakes).

Having a map that shows the contour of the lake bottom (these are sometimes available locally) is a big help. Submerged structure frequently indicates where trout will be suspended, though sometimes many feet above the bottom. One of the chief reasons large trout hang out over structure is because their sources of food are often sheltered down below, venturing out to feed only at night or on overcast days. Types of forage include smaller gamefish, minnows, highly-adapted aquatic insects and even zooplankton.

Another good way to define a lake's structure is to observe objects such as large points and follow their logical course out into the water. Points, shoals and reefs often extend for hundreds of yards, perhaps miles on large bodies of water, as they gradually decline beneath the water. These large points are natural fish magnets.

Of course, the most predictable method is to use sonar which will graph trout locations for you. In large lakes, this can still be a time-consuming process. Narrowing the search area using the above methods means more time fishing.

It's almost like deep-sea fishing when an angler goes after trout that are escaping warmer water near the lake's surface.

One thing that holds true, again especially for lake trout, is that in the winter when the fish are "actively" feeding, they will tend to be farther down in the limnetic zone where, because the lake has turned over, the water is warmer. Although this water is still quite cold, the difference in temperature is sufficient to increase the metabolism in the cold-blooded creatures which encourages them to pursue prey instead of holding in a suspended torpor.

This middle zone has its "peak" periods during the heat of summer when trout drift down to escape warming water temperatures that are approaching lethal levels. Fishing in the middle zone improves again in winter when shorelines and other shallow areas freeze-up and oxygen levels begin to plummet. At greater depths, there is still sufficient dissolved oxygen to carry the fish through a harsh winter.

Lake Bottoms Provide Shelter

With the exception of the bottom environment found in shallow or littoral zones, the area discussed here refers to deep water, including portions of the middle zone where depths are too great to allow the growth of rooted plants. However, enough light still is available in order to allow other types of plants to exist and often flourish.

In the dead of winter in the north country, this profundal zone can be a sanctuary for trout. The water is warm enough to contain adequate (just barely in certain cases) food supplies and oxygen. In shallow and medium-depth lakes, fish kills often result when snow and ice covers the surface so deeply that insufficient light, if any, passes through to the water to allow the regeneration of oxygen. Ice-out leaves a lake surface littered with dead trout and forage fish.

Trout are fish of opportunity. Except at times of spawning when all other activities are suppressed, their top priority is to obtain nourishment. To eat is to grow larger. To increase in size is to reduce the number of predators. The fish do not think in these terms. Evolution just made this a real life fact. Anytime trout can pick up a relatively safe meal, instinct takes over and they do so. During the high-intensity, high-exposure periods of daylight hours, there are not many areas offering these conditions. The bottom zone is one of them.

In deep lakes, over 150 feet, light cannot reach the bottom and no plants will grow. In many respects this is a dead zone and few trout will be found. There is little in the way of food to attract them. Outside of lake trout, other species rarely will be found at these depths. Actually, in most cases, far less than 150 feet is the cutoff point for most trout. This depends a good deal on water clarity. Waters such as Lake Tahoe are extremely clear, free of any particles to refract and diffuse light, so that trout can be found deeper than 150 feet. This is an exception, though. Trout bodies do not handle the extreme pressures associated with these depths and their food sources are not found in significant numbers in these areas. Again, there are always exceptions such as steelhead in the Great Lakes; rainbows, browns and cutthroats in some of the Western lakes and reservoirs; and a few populations of trout living in the Northeast.

This river inlet on Lake Superior in northern Minnesota is an example of the habitat and haven that is offered to trout.

Basically, lake bottoms are relatively barren areas devoid of food and, therefore, trout. The major exceptions (excluding shallow water areas) are those with uneven or jagged contours below areas where fish normally suspend during the day and the deepest points in shallow to medium-depth lakes during the winter. Truly deep water is not true trout water.

Inlets And Outlets Concentrate Fish

If there is such a thing as a "sure thing" when it comes to finding trout in a lake, that item would have to be an inlet, with lesser emphasis accorded an outlet. Water entering a lake from a river, stream or creek offers trout cool habitat and a ready source of abundant and varied food. Anything that washed or fell into the water upstream and was not eaten by river dwellers in passing, normally enters the lake at the inlet.

Tons of silt, sand and fine gravel are also deposited, forming deltas and gravel bars. These are usually too shallow to hold trout, but just off the edges in deeper water the trout will be holding, waiting for food to wash over from above. Because these spots are deep, trout will be here all day and all year if there is any flow at all in winter.

As a result of the high levels of oxygen found in this moving water, all sorts of nymphs will be present, scampering along the bottom, over rocks and underneath them along with being buried in the streambed. Trout will root around with their snouts looking for these morsels along the drop-off during daylight. If concentrations of insects are good in the shallow water above, the fish will move up onto the deltas themselves at dusk or early in the morning.

In the calmer areas, off to the sides of the main flow, forage fish will also be taking advantage of the aquatic insects, and trout will be taking advantage of these. Eddies will concentrate any dead food sources trapped in the current, particularly terrestrials like ants, crickets and grasshoppers that, because of their body structure, tend to float for long periods of time. Trout likely will be found feeding under these concentrations.

For as far as seams and ripples of current are visible in the lake, trout will be found feeding on objects delivered by the flow. At the inlet of large rivers, this can be a mile or more. In most streams, the distance is measured in hundreds of feet. Very big fish will work these areas, preying on smaller fish (in big lakes this could mean trout or whitefish of 12 inches or more being attacked by much larger members of their own clans).

Depending on the species, spring and fall are also times of trout concentrations around outlets as the fish gather in preparation for their spawning runs upstream—rainbows and cutthroats in the spring; browns, brookies and bull trout in the fall. Large numbers of trout are present at these times, but their feeding cycle is at a low ebb as the breeding imperative takes over. The trout are already territorial and will begin to drive away intruders from established holding areas. Any feeding at this time is incidental.

Outlets Connect Habitats

Trout never seem to do any moving through their specific environments in smooth, consistent patterns. They always shift from habitat to habitat in stages, moving to a different area then waiting days or weeks before moving again.

Outlets are basically doors that are open between rivers and lakes. When streamflows diminish and warm as summer progresses, trout are forced to seek shelter, and this often means moving up out of rivers and into the deeper, cooler water found in lakes. Just outside lakes at these times, the fish will concentrate in any pools or deep runs that can shelter them before they plunge through the shallow water and into the lake. Once in the lake, they will stay below the outlet for some time.

Once acclimated to their new environment, the trout will begin actively feeding on the usual gang of suspects present—forage fish, aquatic insects, scuds, terrestrials. Because the fish have often been stressed by the declining environment of their home streams, they frequently go long periods without consistent nourishment and then begin a period of feeding steadily and aggressively.

Lakes and reservoirs are decidedly different habitats than rivers and streams, but there are similarities that help the angler find trout and their food sources with consistency.

A flat lake surface resembles a pool in a river. The most productive areas on lakes always have some form of structure, whether it be weedbeds, rocks or upwelling springs which create the movement or chemical reactions that provide the necessary oxygen for trout. Large, wide-open parts of pools are normally barren of trout, too. Shelter from predators is a prerequisite.

In deeper water, the natural actions of the elements and even the earth's rotation create subtle currents along and around reefs, shoals and boulders that attract the fish. Any situation that creates similar conditions found in rivers and streams is a good place to find forage fish, insects, crustaceans and other food sources, or temperatures, that draw in trout. When fishing lakes and reservoirs look for these variations in what is, in reality, a vast, barren, liquid desert.

=11=

Spring Creeks

Forget everything you have read up to this point concerning finding trout and their food sources. Well, almost everything. Compared to rivers and streams or lakes and reservoirs, spring creeks are considered a different animal entirely.

Spring Creeks are found throughout the country from the fertile limestone regions of eastern Pennsylvania to the streams of southwestern Wisconsin, on out west to some wonderful creeks in Wyoming, Idaho and Montana, and in almost every other state, for that matter. Wherever clear, cold water bubbles come up of the ground in adequate volume to create a creek, you have the makings for a quality trout environment. They are a universal, trout-filled and exceptionally difficult-to-fish phenomena. That's for sure.

Spring Creeks Provide Stable Conditions

These are streams that exhibit extremely stable environments. They are rarely subjected to floods or even high water. Their temperatures remain stable to within a few degrees because most of the streamflow is from underground springs. Currents are relatively constant throughout the length of the creek with variations measured in tenths of a mile and not miles per hour as with other rivers and streams. In England, spring creeks are known as chalk streams and much of our present-day knowledge concerning angling for trout, particularly with a fly,

The perfect scene is an angler with a sharply-bowed rod and a good fish on line. The far shore, especially in and around the partially-submerged logs and clumps of plant growth, is an excellent place to look for large trout.

Spring Creeks   121 has resulted from hundreds of years of experimentation and experience on these chalk streams.

The springs pour in dissolved gases, notably carbon dioxide and dissolved nutrients ideal for green plants, and make for a fertile habitat that is characterized by dense weedbeds of watercress and similar plants. This abundance of plant growth creates a rich environment that is self-sufficient. The resident insects do not have to depend on other organic matter such as leaves and grass to provide additional nutrients.

Trout That Behave Like Elk

Tom Rosenbauer of The Orvis Company refers to trout in spring creeks as being "much like elk grazing in a meadow" because of their tendency to roam around in search of food instead of feeding from one well-defined holding spot. Because of this richness, trout will be found in dead-still backwaters well away from the main current. Sufficient quantities of insects are available throughout the system's exceptionally clear water. Large trout can be anywhere, often in water bordering on stagnant, feeding on nymphs that can be seen rising through the water by the thousands. This is not a case of one or two or maybe three fish working, but can mean literally hundreds of trout tailing (dipping down toward the bottom to take nymphs) and delicately sipping emerging insects.

Because a trout's diet consists almost entirely of insects in this water, and because of the clear waters, spring creeks are best fished by the fly fisher and, even far less often, baitfishers willing to use extremely small baits and a great deal of stealth. Other methods like casting small spinner or spoons are too disruptive in this glass-house setting, and they will put the trout down, usually for the day.

There are really only a couple exceptions to the statement, "you can find trout everywhere in a spring creek," and at first glance they will seem surprising. On further examination they make infinite sense from a trout's viewpoint. Both pools and riffles are unproductive, rarely holding fish of any size.

Even Mild Currents Undesirable

Even the mild currents required for dredging out a modest pool on a spring creek are sufficiently greater than those

This is a classic spring creek in Montana. Big trout will be holding in the lanes between the weedbeds. A careful approach is absolutely necessary so you don't spook them.

currents found in the rest of the stream. The same holds true for riffles. There is no good reason for trout to forsake the bounty of good food. Enough food is holding in channels between weedbeds or long grassy banks for the trout to move even though it means fighting the current of pools and riffles. An angler is wasting his time in these spots. Plus, 95 percent of the time on spring creeks you are fishing to visible, feeding fish. In fact, on English chalk streams, the process has evolved to a point where it is forbidden on most private waters (and that is about all that is left in England) to cast to anything but a rising trout. The reason for this makes sense, though. Blindly casting to holding water will more than likely spook a dozen trout for every one turned. Obviously, this kind of fishing is not for many anglers.

On other types of water, when an angler finds a creek, stream or other flow entering the area being fished, he will normally find concentrations of trout. This does not hold true on spring creeks because the overall water quality of the creek is so high that tributary flows do not add to water quality, and, as a result, there is really nothing special to attract the fish.

Thick weed growth often divides the current of spring creeks into channels, and these are the most productive fishing regions. One thing to remember when trying to locate the trout (on those rare occasions when they are not visible) is to always try the side of weedbeds that is adjacent to the main current because a greater number of insects can be found.

As current does not often exceed 1.5 feet per second, an angler fishing outside bends in a spring creek will find trout not more than a few yards from the bank. This differs from faster, flowing rivers and streams where the fish are often holding on the inside bend in much slower water, and often much farther from the bank.

Trout Feed At Definite Times

One frustrating fact of life concerning spring creeks is that trout feed at definite times of the day, with activity lasting as little as an hour. This varies from creek to creek throughout the country and also for adjoining spring creeks that may only be separated by a low ridge. Fish may turn on in one stream at, say, 10 a.m. while in another the trout may not begin to feed until 4 p.m. This is all dictated by water temperature. While temperature in these flows remains relatively constant, the sun can increase temperature slightly, increasing both trout and insect activity. This pattern varies from stream to stream and can only be learned by observation and by taking temperature readings. The warmer the flow, the earlier in the day the trout begin moving around in search of food.

(Spring creeks are essentially anomalies as trout waters when compared to other habitats, so specific angling information will be discussed here, while techniques for the other types of water will be dealt with in later chapters.)

Clear Water Requires Stealth

With the exceptionally clear water associated with spring

creeks, stealth is as important as the offering. Rarely can an angler approach closer than 25 feet. Based on light refraction, if you are 6 feet tall and a trout is holding 2 feet below the surface, you had better be at least 36 feet away from the fish you are after. Rosenbauer refers to this as his "rule of six," where you multiply height above water by six.

Generally, the deeper a trout is holding in a stream the greater the horizontal distance he can see above the surface. Fish feeding and holding closer to the surface can be approached more easily. This is because the trout's angle of vision is shortened and the surface outside this cove is impenetrable, appearing like a mirror reflecting light back to the fish. Surface disturbances such as wind rippling the water break up the sight lines so that you can fish at closer distances without discovery.

This seems like a lot to factor into catching trout, but it is absolutely necessary for taking fish on spring creeks. To ignore these factors is to not catch fish. Actually, this situation holds true on any type of water, but it is much more critical in a spring creek environment.

The size of the fly or bait also is critical to spring-creek fishing. Anything over No. 12 is probably too large, and there are hatches on some creeks in Michigan where fly fishers have dropped down to No. 30, hooks that are so small you could fit a dozen on a fingernail. As is readily apparent, even the baitfisher is out of luck under these conditions.

Matching what is hatching here, or matching the nymphal form, is critical and again varies drastically from stream to stream. Most often, the most important insects are mayflies followed roughly in importance by caddis flies, stone flies, midges and then terrestrials along banks. Experience and observation will help you match your offering to those that trout in a given spring creek prefer. For those new to an area, the only "quick fix" is to inquire at the nearest fly shop or sporting goods store. Where there is a quality spring creek, there is a quality shop. This is an axiom of human behavior when it comes to fishing for trout. Another good source of information, and this holds true for all angling situations, is the local fish and game department. The biologists have information concerning every species of insect present in a stream,

Staying well back from the water on spring creeks is necessary to avoid scaring spooky trout which could be feeding anywhere in these creeks. Remember the trout's cone of vision.

including dates of emergence. Time spent with these people can give you a "cram course" covering a specific stream.

Pheasant Tails Offer Hope

One pattern that has overall applications for spring creeks and will take fish when worked carefully is the Pheasant Tail nymph. The fly imitates a number of species, and when drifted between channels in the weeds or worked through a trout's feeding lane, it will often produce strikes. No one pattern will ever cover all conditions, but the Pheasant Tail is an excellent starting point on unfamiliar spring creeks. Because of the gentle nature of the current, additional weight in the form of split shot or twist-on lead strips is rarely needed. The weight of this pattern is sufficient to drop down to the fish when cast far enough upstream and allowed to dead-drift back.

Casting a fly to these fish generally calls for an upstream presentation that lands well above the feeding trout and then drifts over the feeding lane. Long, fine leaders of 12 feet or more are needed, and even then the fish may spook. Because of the abundance of food, the trout will not move more than a few inches left or right to take a passing insect, including a large one such as a grasshopper. There is just too much food in and on the water to make this necessary. Those who fish extensively on spring creeks often carry hundreds of flies with them that they cast with delicate rods. They have perfected the art of throwing curves and slack in their lines to extend a drag-free float to their flies. If the pattern does not pass over the trout at exactly the same speed as that of the creek's current, the trout will reject the offering and often will spook, heading to the bottom to hide.

As was stated earlier, spring creek fishing is not for all of us. But for many, especially those who find stalking trout and making exacting, delicate casts and measuring success in fooling one or two crafty trout, this type of water is the ultimate challenge. Just remember, those who do fish spring creeks regularly also experience a good percentage of frustrating, fishless days.

=12=

The Great Lakes

The Great Lakes contain over 6 percent of the world's supply of freshwater and some of the finest fishing for steelhead in North America. And all of this has taken place in really the last few decades. Coupled with fishing for brook, brown, lake and rainbow trout (and several species of salmon), the Great Lakes provide one of the largest and most productive fisheries for trout in the world.

Up until the 1960s trout populations in this system were in serious decline, beginning with the opening of the Welland Canal in the 1930s. This shipping lane provided access to ocean creatures including the sea lamprey and the alewife.

Lake trout proved to be a perfect host for the eel-like lamprey. Coupled with the fact that it had no natural predators in the lakes, the lamprey thrived, to say the least. Commercial overfishing also contributed to the lake trout's demise.

In the lake trout's place came the shad-like alewife that quickly multiplied to the extent that by the mid-1950s, the species comprised the bulk of the fish population in the Great Lakes. For all intents and purposes, sportfishing for trout in the lakes was dead.

After an effective poison was developed to help control the lamprey population, the state of Michigan introduced nearly a million coho salmon smolts into the Great Lakes system. After only 16 months in the lakes, the fish had grown to weights of up to 16 pounds, and the experiment led to plantings of other

There's a special excitement when the downrigger releases and you know something has your bait. On the Great Lakes, you're fishing deep and trout don't give up easily.

The Great Lakes

sportfish including trout. Also, with the lamprey under control, the lake trout population rebounded and is an integral part of the Great Lakes sportfisheries today.

Lakes Are Really Two Separate Fisheries

The Great Lakes offer two separate types of fishing—the vast, open spaces of the ocean-like environment that extends for miles and hours from shore, and the fishing found around the outlets of the countless rivers, streams and creeks that pour into the lakes.

When you consider that Lake Superior is the largest freshwater lake in the world, covering 20,352,000 acres, 350 miles long by 160 miles wide and over 1,300 feet deep in spots, you realize that venturing out onto its vast surface is not a frivolous adventure. Make a mistake out there and you will die. Waves as high as 23 feet have been recorded in Duluth Harbor. One shudders to think of the wave size out on the open water.

The system also experiences minor lunar tides or possibly seiches (fluctuations in the water levels of bays and harbors caused by things such as changes in barometric pressure, the wind or earthquakes). In Superior, this activity along with the strong wave action interrupts or prevents the formation of thermoclines. It appears that the body of water is one continuous thermocline extending from shore to shore. This greatly increases the difficulty of finding trout since there is no specific layer of water for the angler to key on.

Open Water Is Invitation To Disaster

"Because of fierce storms that can quickly develop and the many navigational hazards that exist, pleasure boating on Lake Superior should be undertaken with extreme caution."

This warning taken from the publication "Surface Water Resources of Bayfield County," published by the Wisconsin Department of Natural Resources, states sound advice for all five lakes.

So, basically, fishing out on the lakes is for the experienced charter boat captain or seasoned local angler who is familiar with the water. Lake trout concentrations in deep, offshore waters lure many anglers to the wide open spaces of these great lakes, and on Lake Michigan, steelhead congregate along

Having a laker this size to show for your efforts is a major reward when you're fishing the Great Lakes. There's a lot of territory to cover in finding them.

mid-lake temperature breaks along the surface where they are consistently taken.

River Outlets Prime Locations

The areas around the outlets of rivers and streams which feed the Great Lakes comprise a unique environment unto themselves. This trout habitat does not have a true likeness anywhere else, including larger lakes found in the Northeast or way out West. Most large, inland lakes are drops in the bucket by comparison to the Great Lakes, and that accounts for the major difference in the fisheries and the size of the trout. The old axiom, "big water, big fish," holds true on the Great Lakes and might even be modified slightly to say, "huge water, sometimes huge fish." The forces that drive this system and the fish that inhabit these waters have combined to create a different set of variables. The closest comparisons are with the sea-run browns of the Atlantic Ocean and the steelhead of the Pacific Ocean, but there are many differences, too.

Great Lakes Trout Run Larger

A 5-pound trout is a good fish anywhere and a 10-pounder out West is serious business, but in the Great Lakes fish this size

Working The Concentrated Food Sources

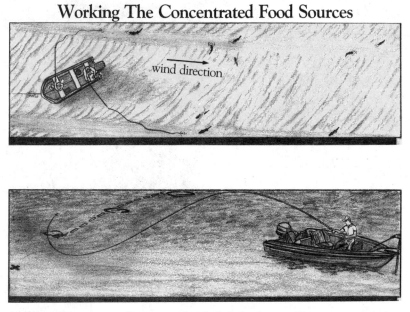

Since rising lake trout usually cruise as they feed, the angler must learn to correctly estimate the trout's feeding pattern and time his casts accordingly.

are not uncommon even when fishing rivers and streams. True, the steelhead do not grow as large as their coastal brethren, but they do top 20 pounds regularly and the other species pass 5 pounds like it was standing still.

Almost any stream entering the Great Lakes has the potential to offer top-notch fishing for trout. Waters that never had runs of trout or, at best, very small ones now are trophy fisheries. A prime example is Wisconsin's Door County where a number of small streams enter Lake Michigan and have good runs of large steelhead. Hooking a 20-pound fish in a stream only 25 feet wide is something of a challenge—which is something of an understatement. The species spawns in the spring and has a false run in the fall when they do not spawn. With the introduction of the Skamania strain of steelhead, there is also a summer run of fish that often exceed 15 pounds in size. Brooks, browns and a very few lake trout move into these tributaries in the fall.

There are specific conditions that trigger fish movement upstream. Prior to this, they will begin to gather or stage at the mouths or in the bays of the tributaries. When water temperatures climb from the upper 30s and into the 40s, steelhead will begin moving into the streams. If this event coincides with a heavy rain that significantly raises stream levels, the run will be on in earnest, and the fishing can sometimes be excellent.

Lake Erie May Be Most Fertile

Of all of the Great Lakes, Lake Erie is by far the most productive fishery from the standpoint of biomass (the amount of living material in a system). This does not mean that it is the best lake for the trout fisher, and much of this abundance is walleye, perch and rough fish. Based on two methods of determining productivity—commercial fishing success and percentage of shoal (shallow water)—the lakes rank this way: 1. Erie, 2. Huron, 3. Michigan, 4. Ontario, 5. Superior.

This does not mean that Superior should be ignored when it comes to catching trout. In fact, because of the remoteness and relatively light fishing pressure, many of Superior's tributaries are considered among the best in the Great Lakes. To give one brief example, the Brule River is justly famous for its inland trout fishing but is now experiencing healthy runs of steelhead and browns. Many north shore tributaries have runs of steelhead, brook trout and brown trout.

Probably, most of the big trout are being taken from the Canadian tributaries of Lake Huron, but so many streams offer quality fishing that rating waters in most cases is a matter of seeing "how many angels can dance on the head of a pin."

Other Fish Are Primary Food Source

Food sources for trout in the Great Lakes are primarily in the form of forage fish and include alewives, smelt, chubs, perch, herring, cisco, whitefish and minnows. These forage species are important for trout when found in association with the estuarine environment commonly associated with the open water of bays where rivers and streams enter the lakes. This habitat is similar to that found where rivers enter the Pacific Ocean along the Oregon and Washington coastlines. The forage fish can sometimes be found short distances up the tributaries, but these are not good locations to find large trout except during early spring or late fall. Low-water conditions

Streams such as this one feeding into Lake Superior have a beauty all their own. As these fishermen indicate, these streams also are good sources of trout.

make migration of large salmonids difficult or impossible most of the year and trolling the bays is far more productive than searching streams.

Trout will be found roaming throughout rivermouth areas but are often concentrated along breakwaters, piers, on the lakeside of sandbars, at the mouths of tributaries, along rocky points and down around reefs and shoals.

One productive technique for lake trout used primarily in the spring just after ice-out is to fish with a dead smelt for bait. This is done from shore by casting the smelt into 20 to 40 feet of water and letting it settle to the bottom. A slip sinker is connected to the line above the hook and moves freely back and forth along the line allowing the trout to grab and run with the bait without feeling the drag of the sinker. An open spool must be used to allow line to flow off the reel freely when a lake trout hits the bait and runs out from shore with it. The technique is particularly effective around points. As soon as the water begins to warm toward summer levels, the lake trout leave the shallow water and head for deeper, cooler regions.

In Great Lakes feeder streams, aquatic insects do not play as significant a role as they do in other trout waters because of the trout's large size. Trout in these streams are mainly on spawning runs, but will feed on forage fish, large aquatic insects, worms, frogs and big terrestrials. These trout rarely rise to surface insect activity and many hook-ups are a result of the fish displaying a territorial instinct to try to drive away or eliminate intruders. Any large lure used by the angler at these times should provoke this aggressive behavior.

Resident Trout Provide Action

There are also resident trout populations (fish that remain in streams and rivers all year) in Great Lakes tributaries, but while they provide sport and, in other parts of the country, may be of sufficient size to consist of the primary fishery, some anglers in this region consider them "baitfish." They are an excellent quarry for the ultra-light spin fisher or the fly fisher who uses light tackle. Also, a number of these tributaries have barriers or dams that block the passage of trout upstream, and fish ladders have only partially solved this problem. In these particular streams, resident trout make up most of (or the entire) gamefish population.

Mayflies are the most prolific of the insects in the tributaries, but caddis and stones also have their moments in the sun. A number of these tributaries flow through clay soils and even during low water will appear milky and unfishable. This is not the case. The trout have adapted to the conditions and feed actively on aquatic insects and terrestrials (notably hoppers and crickets in the summer). Due to the milky conditions, the trout are secure from predators flying above and can be taken throughout the day. Resident fish reach good sizes in these waters.

Jassids Can Be Hot

Another insect worthy of the fly fisher's attention in these

You don't always have to be out in the deepest water to catch laker lunkers like this one. Trout come in to hang around tributary inlets to forage on food that is swept into the lake by the stream.

Complete Anglers Library

tributaries is the jassid, which is a terrestrial creature, namely a leafhopper. When at rest, the insects's large wings are folded back along the body much like a caddis, but they are decidedly more pronounced. Body sizes of this species are comparable to No. 16 to No. 28 hook sizes. When these insects are present, because of their distinctive configurations, they are easy to spot and identify. Trout key on leafhoppers and are susceptible to their imitations.

The best method of fishing these insects is to plop them in the water next to the bank. The less-than-delicate presentation attracts a trout's attention in the same way a natural would when it inadvertently lands in the water. Then, allow the imitation to float high in the current as close to the bank as possible. The fish will do the rest.

A World Of Trout-Fishing Opportunity

The Great Lakes offer an angler the chance to catch really large trout either close to shore or in rivers and streams in what is essentially a freshwater ocean environment. The bays, shoals, points and reefs of these lakes are excellent locations to try from boats. Rivers and streams can be fished by boat, wading or from shore to intercept migrating fish or resident trout.

Whatever the method used, much of the fishing along the Great Lakes is readily accessible, allowing the angler a legitimate chance to take a trophy fish without traveling thousands of miles and spending lots of money to reach the remote waters of the world.

Tackle For Trout

13

Rods, Reels And Lines

Fishermen love the tackle that is associated with the sport. They are gadget freaks—collectors of rods, reels, lures, flies, hooks, sinkers and any other fishing paraphernalia they can get their hands on. Even if they, for some terrifying reason, were not allowed to fish anymore, they would still enjoy their fishing gear. In the dead of winter, when it is even too cold to step outside for a couple of hours and go ice fishing, pulling a cherished reel or beloved rod out of storage and twirling the handle or false casting in the living room brings spring and a new fishing season that much closer to reality. Admittedly the family hound may look upon this indoor angling with skepticism—but then, that's life.

The level of angling sophistication throughout the country has never been higher. People will no longer accept shoddy equipment. There are just too many determined companies out there marketing very impressive equipment.

One cannot argue with the intrinsic beauty and the craftsmanship that are so obvious in a fine bamboo rod that took someone hundreds of hours to make. On the other hand, no one can argue either with the fact that today's graphite rods out-perform those wonderful cane rods by a country mile. The same holds true with today's reels, and with the new synthetics that produce stronger yet thinner lines.

Perhaps the one area where tackle for catching trout has not changed significantly in the past few years is in lures, flies and

A balanced outfit is only part of the equation for a serious trout fisherman. Hat and glasses to protect the eyes and head, waders, a fishing vest and net round out the package.

Rods, Reels And Lines

live bait. Sure, there have been some improvements in materials and finishes and maybe even in the quality of steel in some makes of hooks, but overall what caught fish 25 years ago still catches fish today, and just as successfully. Manufacturers can put lights and whistles and bells on the lures, but these contrivances are really variations on the old piscatorial theme. And seriously, how can you modify an earthworm or a can of corn. This is tinkering with perfection and frowned upon by those far above us.

Aside from the significant improvement in materials found in rods and reels (and waders, too), the biggest change in tackle is in the number of businesses which provide you with the best and the latest in gear. Despite some high prices for top-of-the-line items, it is a buyer's market. Properly cared for, today's tackle will last several lifetimes.

Keep In Mind The Intended Design

There are really only three basic types of trout fishing rods—spinning, baitcasting and fly fishing. All others, including mooching and noodle rods are effective adaptations of these basic designs. Each set of rods has reels specifically designed for them and for the unique conditions for which they were intended. The same is true for lines, though with these, and also rods and reels, properly matched quality gear will perform well under a variety of conditions for both small and large trout.

One last thing, while spinning and spincasting are different in some respects, overall they are essentially the same in one key way—both systems make use of fixed-spool reels. For this reason, it was decided that they will both be discussed in the same section of this chapter.

Spinning—A Method For Many Conditions

Both spinning (open-face) and spincasting (closed-face) reels have their advantages. For the beginner or novice, spincast reels are easier to use. All you do is push down on the lever at the rear end of the reel with the thumb of your casting hand and then release it when the target is in line with the rod tip. This, in turn, releases the line to free-spool toward its targeted destination.

With a spinning reel, you trip or pull back the bail, and

Making The Bow And Arrow Cast

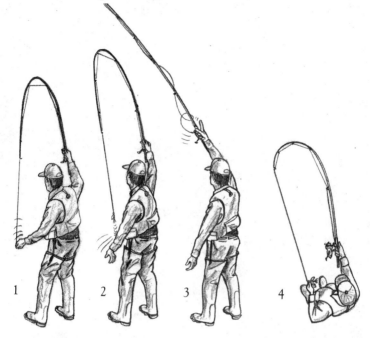

The bow-and-arrow cast, either overhead (1-3) or as a side cast (4), is a neat trick for making a cast in tight areas such as brushy banks or under overhanging branches. Drop lure (1) about 30 inches from rod tip, pick up line with index finger, release pick-up mechanism. Hold hook between thumb and forefinger, extend rod hand and pull back lure to load rod. Take aim and release lure (2) but do not drop index finger. Let outgoing lure (3) snap line from finger.

using the hand that grasps the rod, hold the line in check in the crook of your index finger. When the target comes into sight, you release the line. This is not complicated but does take a good deal of practice to perform accurately, particularly in windy conditions. The advantage to a spinning reel is that you can control the distance of the cast easier by varying the pressure on the line. Both systems are equally effective and have their adherents. Spinning reels are mounted below the rod, while spincast reels are on top of the rod. Spincast rods have a pistol grip that you hold with your forefinger for control during casting. Spinning rods have basically smooth grips and you place your forefinger ahead of the reel stem on the grip, which is often cork.

As just stated, all three types of tackle can be used for

This is the correct hand and fingers position for holding the rod in casting a spinning outfit. This shows how the index finger controls the line prior to release for casting.

fishing for all sizes of trout in all types of conditions, but if limited to only one method, the best choice would be spinning. Given the right rod and reel, an angler can fish the Great Lakes in a gale or cast tiny spinners dead tight to the bank of a clear, meadow stream. Spinning gear can be used to troll, work bait and drift nymphs. Try casting a spoon with a 4-weight fly rod, but be prepared to duck and watch your backside. You can even cast a fly with a spinning reel if you use a clear plastic bubble attached to the line above the pattern, and this can often be a deadly method.

For each class of rod-reel combinations, spincast setups will weigh slightly more than their spinning counterparts because of the heft of the pistol grip and slightly bulkier reels. Both types will handle similar angling situations. Rods range in size and weight from ultra-light to light to medium to heavy with subtle variations in-between.

Defining The Parameters

Ultra-light gear works well on smaller waters such as creeks and streams and lakes and ponds where some degree of delicacy in presentation is required. Fish up to 2 pounds are great sport on this gear, especially in fast water on 2- or 4-pound-test line. These rods are between 4½ and 5 feet in length and weigh less than 2 ounces. The reels are equally small weighing less than 6 ounces in most cases.

Next up are lightweight rods and reels. These rods are usually from 5½ to 6½ feet and handle 6- to 10-pound line. They can weigh anywhere from 2 to 4 ounces. Reels weigh a little more than ½ pound. This size system will handle small- to medium-sized rivers and most lake conditions.

The advantage to both lightweight and ultra-light gear is that their lack of weight helps reduce arm fatigue during a long day of casting, and fish provide greater sport. Disadvantages are that they cannot cope with big rivers and lakes, especially when the wind kicks up. Large trout and steelhead will smash this tackle on the first bruising run. You must match the gear to the water and size of trout being fished.

Medium-weight tackle can be anywhere from 5 feet 9 inches to 8 feet 6 inches in length (for specialty steelhead rods) and weigh between 4 and 7 ounces (or a little more). Line strengths are in the 8- to 17-pound range and reels to handle these run from ¾ pound to 1 pound. This gear is for big water and big fish but still offers some of the sporting qualities that lightweight equipment does.

Heavy rods run from 7 feet to more than 9 feet and weigh at least 5 ounces and often more than 7. Reels are big, serious affairs designed to handle large-diameter lines in the 20-pound range and large fish. Reel weights are over 1 pound and sometimes 1½ pounds. This is bigtime tackle for the toughest conditions on waters like the Great Lakes and along the Pacific Coast where the angler expects to tie into fish weighing 20 pounds or more. Casting these setups for even a couple of hours makes an angler think he will need shoulder surgery.

Line Selection Is Wide Open

There are a variety of monofilament lines to fill the spools of these reels and they come in many colors from clear to blue, green, brown, pink and now fluorescent yellow and green. On quiet, clear waters, pick the line that will blend in best with the water conditions and the weight that matches your rod-and-reel combination. On overcast days or in fast, heavy or choppy water, the bright lines have the advantage of visibility which helps in seeing the take of a trout and in keeping track of the fish as it knifes through the water following a hookup.

Manufacturers are now touting their new thinner-diameter lines. These are great for intense-light, clear-water, spooky-fish situations, but in the lower pound test weights these lines have a nasty habit of tangling at just the wrong time which can be most of the time. In many cases, the "old-fashioned" thicker lines, which are still readily available, are much easier to work, more durable and show up better when used in low-light conditions or on broken-water surfaces. This can be a big plus in detecting subtle takes.

Baitcasting Has Variety Of Uses

The first rod and reel many anglers fished with was a spincasting outfit, and on it, they caught bullheads, sunfish, bluegills, redhorse and anything else that lived in the waters of their youth.

Equipment in this area has advanced by light years. Fully understanding how to use a new baitcasting reel is a complicated process that takes some time and practice. The newly designed graphite rods provide an action, feel and touch that was unheard of even 10 years ago. The level of technological sophistication has advanced to the point where an angler can purchase a setup that will allow him to fish for trout of a couple of pounds and have a dandy time doing so, and then take the same gear and fish for muskies and have a good time doing that.

Baitcasting gear is versatile and durable and, in the right hands, an effective method for taking trout. For casting medium to heavy lures and baits in tough conditions or on big water, these outfits are the first choice for a large number of experienced anglers. They cannot be beat.

Rods Are Strong Yet Sensitive

Baitcasting rods have had the reputation of being so stiff and stout that you could fend of the charge of an enraged Buick with one. This exaggeration is nowhere close to reality today. The rods are strong and designed to handle the antics of any

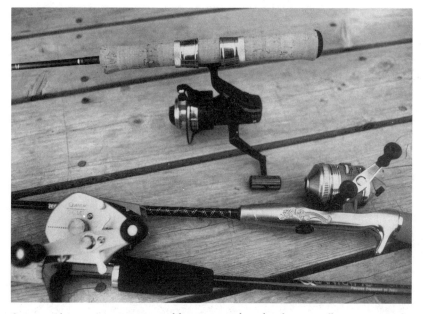

Spinning (from top), spincasting and baitcasting rods and reels are excellent equipment for catching trout. This equipment happens to be made by Zebco.

freshwater gamefish, but most of them are also lightweight, flexible and a delight to cast and play trout with. They come primarily in medium to heavy designs, but even so, they weigh-in between 4 and 7 ounces, with few exceptions on either end of the scale. The pistol grip has become pretty much standard in the industry, but variations of the basic grip have yet to pass the test of angling time.

Baitcasting reels are a marvel of engineering and marketing. To hold one in your hand is to experience technological wonder. Whether the finish is jet black or space-age silver, the reel is beautiful and designed to last for years, given proper care.

In some reels, magnets are used to prevent backlash and the system can be set for an infinite number of conditions. Push-button spool releases, level winding and simplified drag settings are standard on many reels, as are stainless steel ball bearings, spool tension controls (to further reduce backlash) and anti-reverse setups to prevent busting your knuckles when a big fish heads off for parts unknown once it feels the bite of the hook. In short, the reels allow the angler to fish at a level formerly inaccessible.

Fly rods and reels come in an abundance of sizes to suit all needs. Orvis equipment (from top) includes HLS Rounder 7-weight with D-XR reel for big river conditions; 8-foot 3-inch Tippet with matching CFO reel for spring creek conditions; and The One Weight with matching line and reel for extremely finicky trout in clear-water conditions.

Fly-Fishing Gear Selection Is Endless

In no other area of trout fishing is there a greater, more bountiful selection of rods and, to some degree, reels than fly fishing. There are so many rods on the market that sometimes it seems that some of them were made for specific rivers (and indeed a couple were, originally).

Fly rods are defined by two measurements and one slightly subjective characteristic—length, line weight and action.

Line weights begin at 1 (the lightest) and continue past 12, which is well beyond any practical application for the trout fisher. Lengths vary from 6 feet to past 11, though the useful range for trout is 6 through 10. Rod actions vary from *fast-* or *slow*-tip actions (the rod bend is in the final few feet of the rod) to *parabolic* (meaning the flex of the rod is carried throughout the length of the rod) and *typical*, which is something of a combination of the two. Most rods are two-piece items, and a few are three. Most travel rods are four-piece and some custom rods are one piece which are difficult to carry with you—unless lugging 8 feet of rod case through an airport is your idea of quality relaxation time.

A Rod For All Seasons

One-weight fly rods will handle fish up to a couple of pounds but are designed mainly for small, clear waters where careful presentations are required. There is even a 1-ounce rod on the market that uses 2-weight lines—the lightest fly rod commercially available.

Two-weight rods are made for the same situations and will also throw lines up to 65 feet on calm days. But once even a small breeze kicks up, casting for all but the experienced is difficult, if not futile. Three-weight rods handle heavier flies and fish fairly well on smaller rivers. These lighter rods are extremely popular on the spring creeks found in the East in states like Pennsylvania, Vermont and New York.

Fishing With Sinking Tip Fly Line

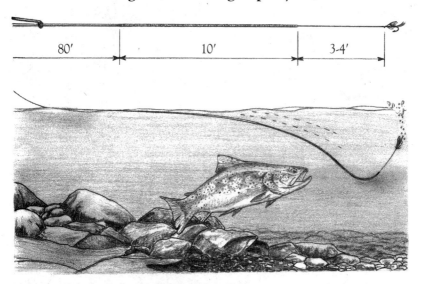

Sinking-tip lines allow a fly fisherman to drop his pattern down to the fish without sinking the entire line which makes retrieving line for another cast more difficult than picking line off the water's surface.

Four-weight rods bridge the gap between smaller streams and full-blown rivers. If put in the right hands, they are a versatile choice.

Five- and 6-weight rods are the ideal all-around selection. They are the most common rods found out West and on the larger waters of the Midwest. These rods, and the appropriate reels and lines will fish big rivers and, with a touch of finesse, will work well on smaller waters.

Seven- and 8-weight rods are for larger rivers, windy conditions, fishing sinking tip lines where backbone is needed to pull the line up from the water to make another cast and for large trout and steelhead work. Nine- and 10-weight rods are big-game rods used for steelhead and sea-run browns, the harsh conditions of the Great Lakes and in extremely windy fishing.

Fly-Rod Hand Grip

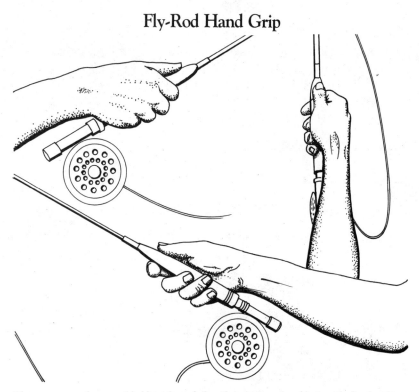

There are several ways of holding the rod, but the most comfortable is with the thumb on top. Keep thumb in line with rod and rod centering the target. Your rod hand should be comfortably relaxed for casts of average distance. The rod will do most of the work; you will simply move it smoothly back and forth.

Basic Fly Line Shapes

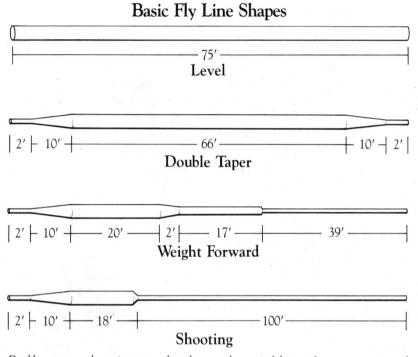

Level

Double Taper

Weight Forward

Shooting

Double tapers are the easiest to mend on the water because of their uniform construction and reduced surface tension. You can also use the other end when the first end wears out. Weight forward casts farther because of reduced line diameter following the thicker floating section. The shooting head is a further refinement of the weight-forward line and is used a good deal for steelhead fishing where long casts are required. These last two lines are difficult to mend because of their tendency to sink and hold in the water.

A day spent casting with these rods is work.

Line Choice Is Varied

Unlike other types of fishing where the weight of the bait or the lure carries the line out to its intended target, fly fishing has the weight of the line doing the work. Fly lines are thick, heavy things to which a leader of monofilament is attached and tapers down to a diameter that is sufficiently small to avoid spooking the trout but large enough to hold the fly and fish during the struggle. Backing, often Dacron, is connected to the back end of the fly line to give additional length for fighting strong fish and also to take up space on the reel so the fly line does not become tightly coiled near its end.

There are level (L) fly lines, double taper (DT), weight

forward (WF) and shooting lines (ST)—all designed for specific and separate applications.

Level lines are the same diameter over their entire length, which is normally 35 yards. Once common, they have fallen out of favor because tapered lines cast much better.

Double-taper lines have a long, level middle section that drops down to a fine diameter at both ends. These lines are a little easier to cast and are more accurate than level lines. They are still the most common, in part because they are easier to pick up off the water. When one end wears out, the line can be reversed with equally good results.

Weight-forward lines have a large-diameter front section tapering to the leader and then a long, narrow section. This narrow line shoots through the rod guides with decreased resistance and through the air with the same results, making longer casts possible. They are not as delicate to cast as double-tapers and are more difficult to pick up off the water because the narrow section "clings" to the water more than the double-taper.

Shooting tapers are special lines perhaps only 10 yards long attached to special shooting lines which resemble thick monofilament spinning lines. These cast extremely long distances but are tough for the novice to use. They are mainly designed for the expert to use when fishing large rivers for species like steelhead.

There is also a triangle-taper line that has a gradual increase in diameter from the leader for about 40 feet, then drops abruptly to a small running line. This line combines the best aspects of the DT with those of the ST.

Many of these lines come with sinking tips (F/S) of anywhere from 5 to 20 feet that allow the angler to sink the fly down to holding trout. They are effective but difficult to pick up out of the water. Sinking (S) lines submerge for their entire length and intermediate (I) lines have a decreased rate of sinking. Using a rod less than 5-weight with sinking line is, more often than not, not worth the trouble.

Leaders Are Critical

If a fly could be attached to a fly line, the presentation to the wary trout would be about as successful as throwing an anchor into a pool or run and then trying to catch a fish from it. That is why leaders ranging from a couple of feet to over 15 feet are used to help make the transition from casting line to fly presentation easier.

Tippets (the end of the leader that connects to the fly) range from 0X (the largest diameter) testing in at over 14 pounds, down to 7X or less than 2-pound test. Some anglers are even using 8X and 9X but this is pushing the "finer" aspects of trout fishing to extremes. These lines resemble delicate spiderwebs that are impossible to work even in good light. Landing a 9-inch trout with them is as much a function of luck as skill.

An extremely general rule of thumb concerning leaders is: *the clearer and quieter the water, the longer the leader.* On some spring creeks, leaders of 15 feet are common and longer ones are used under the most trying of conditions.

On big, rushing rivers when fishing a nymph down deep to large trout, a leader of just 2 or 3 feet is needed.

If there were such a thing, an average leader would probably be 9 feet long, tapering to 3X or 4X. This would cover most river and stream conditions and many lake opportunities. Leaders are sold pre-made in either smooth or knotted form in every conceivable configuration to handle all angling situations. Knotted leaders tend to cast straighter and smoother but are also more prone to "wind knots" and resulting break-offs. At less than two dollars a shot, leaders are somewhat over-priced considering manufacturing costs (less than a quarter) but still a bargain for the angler who does not have the time nor the inclination to tie them.

Mooching And Noodle Rods

Two specialty rods that do not fit perfectly into any of the above categories are noodle rods and mooching rods.

Noodle rods are always over 10 feet long and often over 15 feet. For their length they are relatively lightweight instruments that use small-diameter monofilament line. The advantage of noodle rods is they make it possible to fish with extremely light line, thereby allowing the best action for a lure or bait. Once a big fish is hooked, the rod's supple length makes it possible to land very large fish on the lightest fish.

Spincasting outfits like this UL3 Classic by Zebco allow an angler to work smaller water for smaller trout while providing the angler with plenty of action.

Mooching rods are made in the 8- to 9-foot range using 12- to 15-pound-test line. The reel resembles a fly reel that holds 250 yards of monofilament line. Live or dead bait is used with sinkers fixed in place on the line so when the trout hits the bait and comes to the surface, the sinker does not slide and mask the take. This angling often involves reeling as fast as possible to catch up with the surfacing fish and trying to hook it. This is a popular method for steelhead and salmon on the West Coast.

Tackle Exists For Every Style

Whatever way you fish for trout, there is an array of tackle out there to choose from. The more a person chases trout, the more specialized his tackle becomes. Many anglers have attics or basements full of rods, reels and lines from all three basic disciplines just so they can sleep at night, assured that no matter what conditions they encounter, they will be prepared.

14

Trout Lures

Every dollar the average fisherman ever earned in life could be spent collecting lures and flies. Thousands of them are out there hanging on the walls of your favorite sporting goods store, lurking in drawers of display cases or tempting you from the color, glossy pages of catalogs that arrive with frightening regularity in the mail.

Trout have a capricious nature when it comes to opening their mouths. One day you can catch them trolling a doorknob for a sinker and a flattened tin can with a hook in it for a lure. The next day even the most studious and determined (and skilled) angler will get skunked, royally. We are always looking for the perfect lure or fly—that one piece of hammered metal, or that certain combination of feathers and animal hairs that the trout will find impossible to resist. With the perfect lure in hand, even our own shortcomings will not destroy the offering's effectiveness. Each cast will begin a timeless journey into angling nirvana.

In moments of brief lucidity, those quick and all-too-rare brushes with the truth, anglers know there is no such product available and that there never will be, but this does not keep them from searching in boxes of discarded fishing stuff lying on dusty shelves in pawnshops or studying catalogs with a fervor that never existed in our school days.

This, also, is part of the fun and mystique of catching trout. Heading out to the water with that sure-fire lure burning a hole

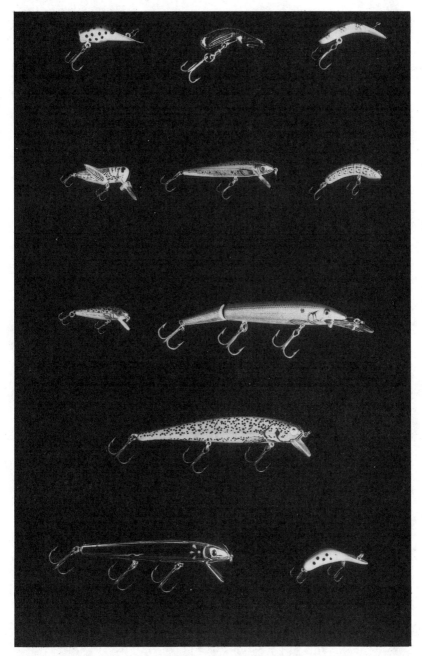

Some popular trout lures include (from top, left to right) Luhr Jensen's Hot Shot, Fire Plug and Kwikfish, Rebel's Crickhopper, Minnow Floater (long) and Cat'r Crawler; Minnow Floater (short) and Fastrac Minnow; Long "A" Bomber, and Cotton Cordel Redfin and Heddon Mini Tadpolly.

in the tackle box, anglers know that a huge trout will hammer the thing on the first, eager cast.

You know what's best about this whole scene? Sometimes the dream becomes reality.

Spinners, Spoons And Plugs

Artificial lures come in so many different styles, shapes, sizes and colors that to suggest that there are 20,000 different ones out there somewhere is to grievously underestimate the facts. There may be 10 times that number, but for catching trout they really break down, once again, into three classes—spinners, spoons and plugs. Everything else for the seeker of trout is that old "variation on a theme" tune.

Native Americans have used hand-carved imitations of minnows and small gamefish for centuries. In fact, a great deal of status was accorded the tribal member who not only could create an imitation that fooled fish, but one that truly resembled the real thing in color, shape and size. Interest in these aboriginal skills is alive and well today with many anglers spending very real money collecting the originals (and, sometimes, fakes).

As to which one of these three categories of lures is the best in terms of taking fish, the race is too close to call. Spinners and spoons are probably about equal overall, with plugs not far behind. Trout do not seem to have any preference in the matter. If any one of these lures is fished properly and directly through a fish's holding area, chances are a strike will be the result. The main criteria for choosing a type of lure is not the species of trout sought, but more the type of water to be fished. If a lure produces enticing action, even if its shape and coloring do not closely match anything presently living in the water being fished, there is still a high probability that a trout or two will show some interest.

There is some truth to the less-than-famous or accurate axiom "the bigger the fish, the bigger the lure used." Big trout concentrate on sizable prey, but many trophy fish have been taken on ¼-ounce or smaller lures. The significant factor is that lures, more than flies or bait, are attractors, meaning trout hit them because the flash, sparkle and zip of the spoon or spinner has triggered the trout's aggressive instincts. This is not to

The ultimate dilemma for a fly fisher is what fly to tie on. This angler ponders the contents of his fly box while mayflies (Hendricksons) swirl through the air around him.

suggest that lures do not imitate trout food sources. They do. Wooden and plastic minnow imitations are consistently among the best-selling lures on the market.

Spinners—Dressed Or Undressed

This type of lure consists of a blade that rotates as it is pulled through the water, along with a body (usually metal) followed by a treble hook which may be either plain (undressed) or with a tail of natural animal hair or feather barbules. As to which one works better, there is no concrete answer. Some anglers swear by one or the other and will fish with nothing else—no exceptions.

A basic approach to selection is to use bright spinners in dark or cloudy water or on overcast days or in low-light conditions. The clearer the water or more intense the light, the darker the lure. While one of the main selling points of a spinner is its ability to reflect light off its rotating blade, too much flash may send trout to cover. If somebody dragged a highly-polished chrome Buick through your living room, chances are that mixed in with healthy quantities of surprise and astonishment would be rushes of adrenalin-powered fear. Also, start out with plain hooks and if these fail to turn trout, switch to dressed versions and repeat the experimentation process just described. Logical and systematic exploration of unfamiliar water or conditions saves time.

The prudent trout fisher carries a number of spinnerstyles in various sizes and colors. Sizes range from $\frac{1}{32}$ (too small for most situations) up to $1\frac{1}{2}$ ounce (suitable for catching world-record, sea-run trout and small, single-engine boats). The most effective sizes are between $\frac{1}{12}$ ounce and $\frac{1}{3}$ ounce. A selection of these in silver and gold along with a few red-and-white, black-and-white and some chartreuse spinners will handle most water. The chartreuse spinner is very good in late summer and early fall when spawning species like the browns and brookies are on the move.

Spoon-Fed Trout

There are a least as many spoon designs and color patterns as there are different spinners. Spoons have gold, silver or copper finishes in plain or hammered metal. They may be painted in the classic (and extremely useful) red-white-red scheme or colored to imitate frogs, minnows, other trout or an Arizona desert sunset. If a person had 500 different color combinations, he might have approximately half of those available to anglers.

Spoons ranging from $\frac{1}{4}$ ounce to 1 ounce in weight are the most popular for the caster. Weights of over 3 ounces are often used by trollers.

Many of these spoons do not really look like the standard lure, one does indeed resemble a teaspoon. Trolling spoons, or flutter spoons, are oblong pieces of thin metal that are almost flat on both sides. Wobblers resemble spoons. They are useful for trolling, but the weight of many wobblers makes them more suitable as casting lures used for the same situations where

This selection of metal spoons is the author's favorite for taking trout. Of the group, the red-and-white spoon (lower right) still works best. Trout seem to prefer the color contrast.

standard spoons could be used. Some spoons are made weedless by the inclusion of a flexible piece of metal that extends from the front of the spoon to cover the hook tip. This simple addition provides a "cover" for the hook point as it travels though weedbeds or even piles of brush; yet is flexible enough to permit penetration of the barb when a fish strikes.

The choice is up to the angler, but a basic selection of spoons would include gold, silver, red-white and black-white in ¼-ounce to 1-ounce weights. These will take trout in most lakes and rivers.

Plugging The Gaps In The Arsenal

Obviously, there are a sufficient number of spinners and spoons to cost a fisherman a small fortune if he so desires, but when his attentions are turned toward the serious collecting of plugs, the angler can be in big trouble. The array of lures available is staggering—wooden minnows, plastic minnows, jointed and single-piece flatfish, barrel-shaped plugs with legs that kick and swim, poppers, deep-diving minnows, plugs with lights and sonic attractors—the choice is never-ending and mind boggling.

The minnow style works well in both lakes and streams, both in floating and sinking forms. The countdown version sinks at a prescribed rate that can be measured by timing its descent, which is helpful when you are trying to consistently work specific levels of a lake. They also give a little more depth for fishing in deep or swift rivers and streams. These imitate forage fish, other trout and some are just plain attractors. Common lengths are 2 through 6 inches. Larger ones are used for trolling.

Wobbling plugs may be used by the caster and can be quite productive on both lakes and rivers. Like flutter spoons, they come into their own as big trout lures on big lakes when trolled deep behind a boat. Downriggers help increase the depth of these lures. Fishermen who pursue steelhead have found wobbling plugs effective when fished downstream into likely holes from an anchored boat.

After these basic, sedate plugs come the legions of "whiz-bang" lures that often feature lights or sonic ringings powered by batteries, plastic frogs or mice with kicking legs and so on. Every tackle box seems to have one or more of these lures. The only action they see on most occasions is when they hook the angler's fingers while he is reaching for something that catches fish.

A small piece of sound financial advice is to, at least initially, avoid lures that require batteries, need winding, have lights, whistles, internal guidance systems or built-in cassette decks. More often than not, these "lures" are over-priced gimmicks dedicated to creating trout terror. It was bad enough when the industry tried to foist electronic reels onto the angling public. Most anglers go fishing to commune with nature and perhaps take a few trout in the process, not to play a riverine variation of "Donkey Kong."

True, some of these odd lures take fish, big fish in large

A good selection of dry flies includes (from top left) the Goddard Caddis, Blue Wing Olive, Black Gnat, Quill Gordon, Trico, Black Caddis, Elk Hair Caddis, Pale Evening Dun and Green Drake Wulff from Orvis.

numbers on occasion, but the time-tested selection described here initially is an angler's best bet. If none of the basic members of the three primary groups takes fish, catching trout with any of the others is casting your lot with fate.

Flies By The Thousands

If you thought the types, sizes and colors of spinners, spoons and plugs was confusing, take a couple of minutes to consider the selection of flies available to the fly fisher. There are dry flies, wet flies, nymphs, streamers, terrestrials, steelhead patterns and combinations of these like legendary flymph, a melding of a wet fly and a nymph.

Add to this jumbled equation hook sizes ranging from 2/0 (the upper limit for most trout fishing) down to No. 32 (well past the limits of decency and visibility for most of us). Don't forget to factor in countless colors, and shades therein, of feathers, synthetic materials, animal hairs, tinsels, threads and a multitude of hook shapes and styles, each designed to make a certain pattern more to a trout's liking.

There are probably 10,000 patterns and designs in use today just in North America. Those guys across the Atlantic or down in South America or Tasmania have a whole different set of patterns that they live and die with on their trout waters. Some of us become so mystified, so caught up in the elaborate layers of flies and fly tying, that all we do is collect and tie flies. We never even go fishing. There is serious madness swirling around the edges of fly fishing.

Dry Flies Are The Top Choice

"Purists" in the pursuit of fly fishing will use nothing but dry flies and look down their self-righteous noses at anyone else using anything but the noble dry fly. The mystique and snobbery surrounding fly fishing has its roots in this narrow discipline that has been a part of trout fishing dogma for a number of centuries.

Still, there is no argument about the excitement of taking a rising trout on a dry fly—watching the fish come to the surface and inhale the fly as it rides perfectly upright on the current or rests serenely on a lake surface. The flies are beautiful, to boot. Crimson, emerald, bright yellow, amber brown, pale dun and royal blue are just a touch of the colors found in dries, which primarily imitate emerging or spent insects.

Some fly fishers have thousands of dry flies, but the following selection, admittedly subjective, will get you started: Green Drake Wulff, Grizzly Wulff, Adams Wulff and Royal Wulff in No. 12 and No. 14; Blue Wing Olive, Pale Evening Dun, Pale Morning Bun and Quill Gordon in No. 14 to No. 18; Black gnat in No. 14 to No. 16; Goddard Caddis in No. 12 to No. 14; Elk Hair Caddis in No. 12 to No. 14; Black Caddis in No. 14 to No. 16; Trico Thorax in No. 20 to No. 22; Light Stimulator in No. 8 to No. 10; and Sofa Pillow in No. 4 to No. 8. Even this small selection, especially when coupled with a selection of wets, nymphs, streamers and terrestrials, represents a serious investment of money.

Wet Flies Fool Big Trout

Wet flies are not as popular as they were 25 years ago but when worked just below the surface they can take some very large trout. Some choice patterns are Cahill, Hare's Ear, Rio Grande King and McGinty in No. 8 to No. 12.

Many times an angler will be fishing a dry fly that has become saturated with water and is now floating in the surface film or just below the surface. Suddenly, the oft-times unproductive dry begins to take trout after trout when fished "wet." As time and knowledge expand, the wet fly will again see a return to popularity, but this is a couple of decades away—nymphs, streamers and dries hold sway these days.

Scuds do not really fit tightly into any one class so both pink and olive ones in No. 14 to No. 18 are good picks. The same is true of woolly worms but they are proven fish takers in olive, black and brown in sizes No. 8 to No. 12.

Nymphs Handle Below-Surface Duties

There are hundreds of nymph patterns, but a half dozen will cover most water successfully. Too many anglers spend too much time deciding what fly to use. You can't catch trout if the fly is out of the water.

The following are good selections: Hare's Ear Nymph in No. 12 to No. 16; Prince in No. 8 to No. 10; Green Caddis Pupa in No. 12 to No. 14; Pheasant Tail in No. 14 to No. 18; Baetis in No. 16 to No. 20; Chironomid Pupa in No. 18 to No. 20.

Two other patterns that are difficult to classify include a Brown Crayfish in No. 4 to No. 6 and a Red Egg Fly in No. 8 to No. 10.

Streamers Pull In The Big Boys

Streamers account for as many trophy fish as any other type of pattern due in part to their large size and often colorful appearance. At least a few of the following should be in every fly fisher's vest:

Muddler Minnow in No. 6 to No. 10; Yellow Marabou Muddler in No. 2 to No. 4; Bark Spruce Fly in No. 2 to No. 4; Olive Matuka in No. 2 to No. 4; Black Nosed Dace in No. 6 to No. 8; Olive and Black Woolly Buggers in No. 4 to No. 6; Brown Sculpin in No. 2 to No. 4; Olive and Black Leeches in

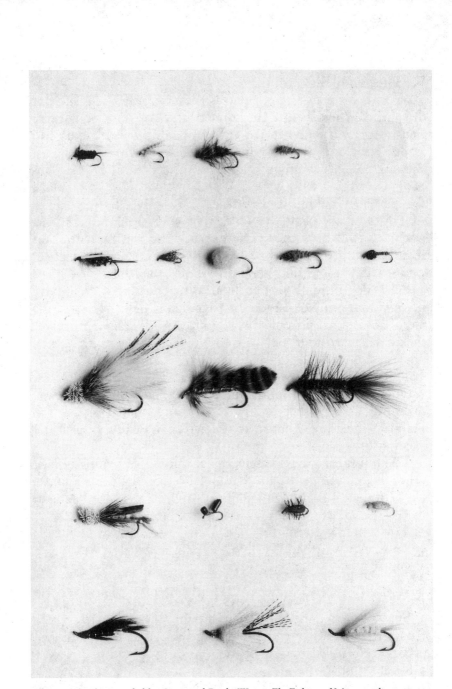

These artificials, provided by Orvis and Bright Waters Fly Fishing of Minneapolis, represent a popular array for trout fishermen. Wet flies (top row) include Black Gnat, Cahill, Woolly Worm and Hare's Ear. Nymphs (second row) are Prince, Caddis Pupa, Red Egg Fly, Western Hare's Ear and Pheasant Tail. Streamers (third row) are Yellow Marabou Muddler, Olive Matuka and Olive Woolly Bugger. Terrestrials include Dave's Hopper, Cinnamon Ant, Black Beetle and Tan Foam Beetle; and Steelhead patterns are Black Bear Green Butt, Chartreuse Krystal Bullet and Polar Shrimp.

Complete Anglers Library

No. 2 to No. 4; Royal Coachman in No. 4 to No. 8.

Bitch Creeks in No. 6 to No. 8 and Girdle Bugs in No. 6 to No. 8 are not true streamers. Rather, they are large nymphs with rubber legs that trout often find hard to resist.

Terrestrials Are A Necessity

Every fly fisher should have at least a few of the following terrestrial patterns. They can turn a fishless outing into a roaring success: Joe's Hopper in No. 8 to No. 10; Dave's Hopper in No. 6 to No. 8; Jassid in No. 16 to No. 18; Black and Cinnamon Ants in No. 14 to No. 18; Black Beetle in No. 14 to No. 16; Letort Cricket in No. 12 to No. 14.

Steelhead Patterns Are Flashy

Steelhead patterns are large, flashy and quite pretty and some of the more popular ones include Babine Special in No. 2 to No. 4; White Wiggle Tail in No. 4 to No. 6; Polar Shrimp in No. 2 to No. 4; Skunk in No. 2 to No. 4; Cowichan in No. 6 to No. 8; Skykomish Sunrise in No. 1 to No. 4; Black Bastard in No. 2 to No. 4.

If you have gone ahead and ordered two or three of each of these patterns in all of the listed sizes, you are now also probably shopping around for the best rates on a second mortgage. The financial burden is admittedly tremendous, but at least you can rest assured that you have a sufficient selection to take trout anywhere in the country, if not the planet.

15

Live Bait

Despite loud claims to the contrary by many anglers who seek trout with lures and with flies, there are an awful lot of times on the water when live bait will out-fish the other two methods, hands down. No question about it.

The obvious advantage to using live bait is whether NAFC members are using worms, minnows or insects, the bait is the real thing. There is no need to try to design the bait to look real like many lures and most flies. This is not to say that fishing live bait is simply a matter of jabbing a worm on a hook, attaching a sinker on the line somewhere and lobbing the whole mess out into the lake in order to start pulling monster trout out of the water. Using live bait is an art just like any other skilled fishing discipline.

And, "live bait" is not always living and breathing and wriggling at the end of the line. It can also be cut or strip bait meaning that a part of a minnow or other fish has been cut and attached to the hook. But, the overwhelming favorite among trout fishers (and all other freshwater anglers) is the earthworm in its many forms. Next in line on the hit parade are baitfish, followed by insects and crustaceans such as scuds and, to a lesser degree, crayfish.

Many experienced baitfishers snell a hook to the line rather than connect it with a knot. Snelling involves (see diagram in Chapter 1, page 14) passing the line through the eye of the

Trout love live food, and minnows and worms are at the top of the list as alluring bait for hungry trout. An inexpensive Styrofoam bucket helps keep the minnows' water at a comfortable level.

Live Bait

Maggots such as these are always great bait for taking trout. They're also sold as a preserved bait, but the live version is always better.

hook and then winding and securing coils along the hook shank. The advantages of this method of connection is that the hook is less likely to hang from the line at an odd angle and move erratically in the water when you are setting the hook. This is critical because this erractic action can have a marked effect on the number of fish you're able to hook.

As for the type of hook to use, there are many. One of the more popular is the baitholder which has two small barbs on the shank near the eye and an offset point which sticks in a trout's mouth with authority when applied by the angler with authority. This is not always the case with other types of hooks. Other hooks include the sproat, which is a good, strong all-around hook and the Carlisle, which is popular with those who use minnows because of its long shank.

Worms Take Trout Anywhere

It is dangerous to make sweeping generalizations about fishing. There are a lot of people waiting out there to shoot you down in flaming embarrassment. But it is safe to say that where trout swim, the use of worms will catch at least a few of them.

Nightcrawlers are large earthworms, and they are used more than any other type of worm. They can be collected at night, using a flashlight in your yard. They will keep for a long time if put in with dry leaves that are lightly sprinkled with water daily. Heavy rains drive nightcrawlers from their underground burrows. Because of this, they work very well when the water is rising on a river or stream, following the heavy rain.

Smaller worms like angleworms can be collected by turning over a shovel-full of soil from the garden or any other location with rich earth. They can be kept alive in loose dirt in a container with airholes punctured in the lid. Smaller worms work well in creeks and small streams and in quiet little lakes.

Whatever size worm used, it should be fished as naturally as possible. This means using hooks in the No. 10 to No. 14 range with as little weight as possible. Trout key on worms drifting freely, writhing in the current or settling naturally to a lake bottom. A large chunk of nightcrawler shoved lengthwise on a hook just does not catch that many trout, especially those trout in wild populations.

Minnows Aren't Bad, Either

Very few trout waters are without some type of forage fish—minnows, sculpins, darters and dace. Where these fish are found, trout will be found cruising in search of an easy meal. Large trout feed heavily on minnows and most wall-mounters are taken on forage fish.

The problem with using live minnows is that they are prohibited in many trout waters. Minnows that escape the hook or are dumped from buckets by anglers may include carp or other young roughfish which survive to spawn, thus populating and eventually harming trout habitat. Some baitfish grow large enough to compete with trout for food. Shiners are notorious for gorging on the aquatic insects that trout prefer. So before using minnows, check the regulations.

Seining streams with fine-mesh nets or using minnow traps

baited with bread or doughballs will provide a day's worth of bait in a short time. These baitfish will stay lively in a minnow bucket immersed in cool water.

Most minnow fishing is done on lakes where the fish are hooked so they are still able to swim around and attract the attention of trout. Another approach is to use the minnows in river shallows next to deep runs and pools where big trout lie in the evenings. The trout move up into the shallows searching for minnows at these times. You will not catch a lot of fish, but they will be large. Just enough weight to keep the minnow positioned in a prime location is all that is required. Because of the absence of current, a single split shot is often all the weight you will need.

The three best ways to hook a minnow and keep it alive and moving are to run the point through the lips, the top half of the tail and through the back just forward of the dorsal fin. The bait should be checked regularly whenever slight movements of the line stop, which may either indicate that the forage fish is dead or that a big trout has swallowed it.

Pieces or entire minnows are often weighted and fished along the bottom of lakes. There are a number of methods for hooking baitfish securely enough so they can be cast and retrieved carefully, or trolled.

Grasshoppers, Crickets And The Like

One of the absolute best baits for taking good numbers of big fish anywhere is the grasshopper. Normally crafty trout lose all caution when these are present in any number on the water. Impaled on a small hook without weight and drifted or "dapped" along the edge of a bank can produce heart-stopping results as the trout rush out from cover to snatch the hopper.

Crickets and, to some extent, beetles also work well. Ants are difficult to hook and never stay on long enough to catch fish with any consistency.

During early morning when the air is still cool and the grasshoppers are slow-moving is the best time to catch them. They can be stored in a ventilated jar that should be kept out of the sun. The best place to hook a grasshopper or a cricket is through the back just behind the head and a short distance in front of the second set of legs.

During the summer, grasshoppers become an extremely important source of food for trout as the insects fly through the air and crash-land on the water. Check nearby grassy fields.

Larvae Trick Trout

The most popular larvae used as live bait is the hellgrammite or dobsonfly nymph. They reach 3 to 4 inches in length and can be easily hooked through the tough collar right behind the head. They can be taken by using a seine and overturning rocks in a stream. They will keep in a minnow bucket filled with moist leaves and some ice cubes to keep the environment cool.

Whether used in a lake or stream, they should be fished close to the bottom but not on it, otherwise they will burrow into the sand or gravel or under rocks. In streams, when they are drifted through runs just above the streambed, they will turn big trout. A bobber adjusted to the stream depth improves the drift technique, or try drifting them with the rod extended out over the run using one hand to hold the line to maintain control and contact with the bait.

Stone fly nymphs and the larger mayfly and caddis-fly nymphs, also work when fished in the same way. Maggots, waterworms, leeches and waxworms also are good baits. They should be hooked behind the head for maximum action.

Trout Dine On Crustaceans

Crustaceans such as scuds and crayfish are always a prime trout food source.

Only the larger scuds have sufficient bulk to take to a No. 14 or smaller hook. No matter how scuds are attached they quickly die, so they are not an active bait. They do have a strong scent which attracts trout. Crayfish swim backward and are best caught by overturning rocks and by driving them into a net downstream. They can be kept alive in minnow buckets. Crayfish can be hooked through the tail or through the carapace just behind the head. Little if any weight is required and the creatures are allowed to crawl along the bottom, with an occasional tug on the line to keep them out of rock crevices where they like to hide.

Mud shrimp are larger, up to 6 inches in length, and are excellent bait for Pacific Coast steelhead. Using a yarn fly combined with the mud shrimp can produce excellent results. The easiest way to obtain mud shrimp is at a bait shop, unless probing the depths of mudflats sounds like fun.

Trout Eat Their Own Eggs

As mentioned in the steelhead section, trout will feed extensively on any eggs present in a stream. Trout will eat them even in waters where eggs are not normally found. These eggs can be impaled on a hook, or several eggs can be lumped together in a 2-inch piece of nylon mesh that is secured with several loops of thread finished off with a series of half-hitches. These egg sacs should be preserved in a jar of borax.

Egg sacs are most effective drifted along the bottom attached to a No. 4 through No. 10 egg hook. In faster rivers a good deal of weight may be required to sink the bait to the bottom. A foot-shaped walking slip sinker works well for this, or a dropper of lesser-strength line can be attached to the rig to hold the sinker. When the weight snags, the dropper will break, preserving the bait.

Tread Lightly With Live Bait

Whatever type of bait a NAFC member uses, he should use the lightest-weight line and the least amount of lead weight possible. The smaller the hook, the better.

Sporting considerations are not the main reason to choose light tackle, though trout will fight better on the lighter gear. The objective is to retain as much life-like or free-moving behavior as possible with both live bait, cut bait and spawn. The more natural and less restricted the drift or float of the bait, the more fish will be caught.

=16=

Miscellaneous Gear

ccumulating gear that is necessary or at least perceived as necessary for the enjoyment and successful taking of trout is a time-consuming and costly process for most anglers. Honestly, how can any angler expect to catch trout consistently without a collection of at least a dozen rods and matching reels, 200 lures, 500 flies and thousands of hooks, sinkers and swivels—most of which have not seen a trout lake or river in several years?

This is a tough sport and it takes more than courage to deal with trout. Waders (both hip and chest in both neoprene and nylon), custom-made wood nets, float tubes and fins, waterproof boots, flexible lights for night side-planing, polarized sunglasses, downriggers and other trolling devices, raingear, fishing mitts, stream cleats, vests, tackle bags, forceps, zingers, creels and, of course, a scale to weigh our trophies—all of this stuff is absolutely essential to a properly conceived angling adventure.

Leave out even just one seemingly insignificant item and the trip is doomed. *The Rhyme of the Ancient Mariner* will seem like a success story compared to the fate awaiting the ill-equipped trout fisher.

"In short, we are a lean, stoic, self-denying crew, always ready to do anything or go anywhere—except home—in our endless quest for trout. Spartanly sacrificing ease, comfort, gracious living—everything—just so long as we can fish. The

A sampling of the author's miscellaneous fishing gear includes felt hat, Barbour Waxed-Cotton Smock, neoprene chest waders, Waterproof camera, vest, landing net, rod case, wading shoes, wicker creel, "Arctic" creel, stream cleats, swim fins for float tubing, neoprene booties and hip waders.

Miscellaneous Gear   177

Pilgrims never had it so rough," explains trout chaser and writer Robert Traver.

Or maybe all of these items are "the tools of ignorance" to borrow slightly from Yogi Berra.

Whatever.

The point is equipment for every conceivable angling need is available. The following is a brief rundown on a small, but important, fraction of the total.

Trolling Devices Expand Your Horizons

Downriggers, side planers, diving planers and the like are all designed to allow an angler to fish water that would ordinarily be too deep, or too far from the boat.

Downriggers are devices designed to troll in deep water for lake trout and other species when they are holding in the depths. The setup consists of a heavy weight, normally resembling a small cannonball, a clip system to hold the fishing line and then release it when the trout strikes (the line jettisons from the weight to facilitate fighting the fish) and a spool to store the weight's line (these often come with gauges or other means of determining the lure's depth). A crank or small electric motor raises and lowers the rig. The whole setup is anchored on the stern of the boat and frequently larger craft have several of these.

When a fish hits, anglers and crew frantically reel in all other lines while the poor soul fighting the fish tries to steer his trout away from the commotion. Many very big trout are taken on downriggers.

Diving And Planing For Trout

Side planers and diving planers are devices that allow an angler to work water well away from the boat in a steady parallel course often 50 to 80 feet distant and well below the surface. Planers allow you to troll a bait or lure through prime water, yet well away from the noise of the motor or shadow of the boat.

Each planer and diver has its own rigging pattern. With in-line planers, your line passes through a swivel or metal-eyed extension, then through or around the planer which is often made of plastic. Some are saucer-shaped, others resemble the fins on an outboard motor. Form follows function with these

A lightweight canoe is an ideal way for a single angler to fish lakes and streams in comfort with relative stability and great maneuverability. However, wear your life vest.

devices. Trolling boards work similarly to side planers, except the fishing line passes through a release so the fish can be fought independent of the trolling board.

In-line planers are attached after you have released anywhere from 50 to 80 feet of line. Then, more line can be released up to 80 feet (though shorter distances seem to work better—less line-drag to cope with). Once the desired distance from the boat is attained, the reel should be locked and set in its holder. An angler can execute two planers or divers, which allows him to work a sizable portion of water both shallow and deep simultaneously.

Hip Deep And Bone Dry

Some of the best trout are taken during the worst weather or in the coldest water. For the angler wading a river, this can mean a day of chilling discomfort or, worse, hypothermia—a condition where the body's temperature drops well below normal. Death can result in severe cases.

Dressing warmly will not help here but wearing waders does. Hip waders cover the legs up to the hips (Surprise!). Chest waders resemble bib overalls in design and are designed for deeper explorations of trout waters.

The two major materials used in wader construction are neoprene (a spongy substance that absorbs water but keeps the angler dry and warm) and nylon (which also keeps you dry but is loose-fitting and bulky). Neoprene fits "skin tight" and can be uncomfortable in warm weather. Many anglers have a lightweight pair of nylon chest waders for summer, neoprene chest waders for cold weather and hip waders for shallow-water work. This can run to over $300. A good choice for starters would be nylon chest waders with boot feet that are simply shoes already built into the waders.

Neoprene, and many lightweight nylon waders, are designed in stocking-foot models requiring the purchase of wading shoes. And, if the waders do not have cuffs, purchase gravel guards that pull on over the waders and then are pulled over the tops of the shoes. This prevents gravel and other material from working between the wader and the shoe, which is uncomfortable and can wear holes in the waders in short order.

For chest waders, especially nylon ones, buy a belt to cinch around your chest to protect against icy water pouring in over the top, and to give you a fighting chance to regain your footing if you should fall down in the stream. Waders left open at the top make great sea anchors and can be deadly in swift current.

Lastly, on freestone rivers that have fast current and streambeds of slippery boulders, stream cleats are a good idea. These are normally rubbers that slip over wading shoes or boots and have doubled bars in v-patterns attached to the bottoms. They greatly improve control in these treacherous conditions. A wading staff is also a good idea in this kind of water.

Float Tubes And Related Contrivances

Float tubes are basically fabric-covered innertubes with seat

A float tube allows an angler to fish high mountain lakes and big high plains waters such as this one with sufficient stealth because it's quiet and the angler maintains a low profile.

harnesses that allow an angler wearing chest waders and swim fins to propel himself backward through the water in search of trout at just slightly higher-than-water level. You always move backward because your kicking action in a sitting position thrusts you in this direction.

Many tubes have backrests, numerous pouches and pockets to hold gear, patches to hold lures or flies and enclosures to secure your rod. They are an inexpensive way ($100 to $200) to fish a lake with stealth and maneuverability. A flotation device should be worn in case the tube deflates.

Another good way to fish a lake by yourself is by using a fishing platform that is really a small-scale version of a float boat. There is a metal frame, two pontoons, a plastic platform for sitting, a small canopy in the back for gear and a space in

Miscellaneous Gear   181 the frame to extend your feet for paddling with waders and fins similar to that of float tubes. The direction of travel is, once again, backward.

Sunglasses Are Good Protection

Whenever NAFC members are fishing with bulky flies or in windy conditions with any gear, they should wear sunglasses. Errant casts or a gust of wind can drive a hook into the eyes.

Also, polarized sunglasses help block out bright overhead and reflected sunlight and give an angler a slightly-improved glimpse into the water to help determine holding areas and even spot trout.

On overcast days when standard lenses prove to be too dark, there are yellow-cast lenses that actually highlight important features on the water while still providing protection from unexpected flying objects.

In the same general category are hats which protect you from hooks and the sun, and a quality sunscreen to limit exposure to the sun. The more exposure and burning over the years, the greater the risk of skin cancer.

Rain Gear Is A Must

So much of the best trout fishing occurs during monsoons and in cold, wet weather that anyone who fishes more than casually should invest in some form of rain gear.

This may be in the form of an inexpensive (and often flimsy) plastic rainsuit or more-expensive waterproof fabrics that "breathe," allowing moisture from the inside to escape. Suits of these fabrics run to a couple of hundred dollars.

For extreme wet and cold, waxed cotton coats and rain pants are by far the most effective and durable. Cotton fabric is soaked in a wax-solution making it impervious to all forms of moisture. This is great stuff for every condition except temperatures below 20 degrees when the material begins to stiffen. The heavyweight garments are too warm for fishing in the summer, late spring and early fall, but lightweight items are also available. This gear is costly but durable.

The Best Of The Rest

Hundreds of other items can be collected for your fishing,

but a few key ones would include a landing net, fishing mittens that have the fingertips cut off to keep your hands warm while still allowing line control, a good pocket knife with nippers or scissors for trimming line, a small first-aid kit for minor emergencies, a waterproof camera (a number are available for less than $200) for proof of catching that big trout you just released, a pocket flashlight for night fishing, tackle boxes, fly boxes, minnow buckets and rubber knee-length boots for working marshy areas or wading in the shallows, and forceps for safely removing hooks from the trout's mouth (and more than likely your clothing, ears, fingers and other sensitive areas).

Obviously, there is much, much more gear lying in wait out there. A good rule of thumb is to begin with the absolute bare essentials, but to buy the best of each piece of gear that you can afford. Add equipment as the need arises. Don't worry. In 10 years, you'll be building a new addition to your home.

Streams

17

Pools

s was seen in the earlier chapter on finding trout in streams, fish will be found in well-defined regions of a river. These locations are fixed by such variables as types of food present, available shelter, time of day, time of year and weather.

The four basic types of habitat found in streams are pools, riffles and runs, banks and fixed objects in the current. Combinations of any, some or all of this quartet along with stream gradient, terrain and geographic location are what produce the countless variations in trout streams.

Moving water also alters a stream course, sometimes overnight, but definitely from year to year. Guides who fish their home rivers more than 100 days a year often mention that they must re-learn a river's secrets at the start of each season. New channels are cut, gravel bars shift or disappear, banks erode, log jams move, disappear or are created—these are only a sampling of the "personality" changes a stream undergoes in the course of a year, and all of these affect trout behavior.

Looking at the kinds of water you are going to fish and analyzing the situation before plunging into the stream, are as important as selecting the proper lure or making the correct casting decision.

The Promise Of Pools

The deep, turquoise water of a classic trout pool is a

Casting tight to structure (in this case a rock ledge) at the head of pools is a good tactic for locating the big trout. Work the area thoroughly without spooking the fish.

Pools

beautiful sight, full of promise and mystery. In this perfect environment, trout of all sizes swim and hold definite feeding positions. More than all other kinds of water, pools are what come to mind for most of us when thinking about fishing rivers and streams.

Pools can range in size from that of a bathtub to more than a mile long and just as wide. They can be a couple of feet deep to 30, 40 feet or more below large dams and beneath falls and chutes of big rivers. Regardless of size, all pools have several basic features in common. Understanding the methods for catching trout on small- or medium-sized streams will allow an angler to take fish on larger rivers.

When fishing a huge river like the Columbia in Washington or the lower Clark Fork in Montana, the idea is to cut the water down to size so you are working a smaller, more manageable portion. Water like that found in the eddies and tails of small pools on California's Hat Creek can also be found on a wide river, but in greater dimension. When trout are rising all over the surface of a pool, size does not matter. You fish to individual rising trout.

Big rivers have small fish and small streams have big fish, but, on the average, the larger the water, the larger the average size of the trout.

Fish From The Tail Up

Optimism is an admirable quality and in fishing it is what often carries us through a tough day. And on outings when we assume the fishing will be great and we know we are going to be on prime water, there are some simple rules to improve our catch rate.

One of the most important rules is to fish upstream. Trout normally face upstream into the current to take any passing food drifting down their way. If you start working a pool from its head on downstream, you will probably take one trout and maybe two, but not likely any more. The fish down below you will have seen and heard the struggles taking place above them which will trigger their instinct to seek shelter. Once this happens, most trout will stop feeding for 30 minutes or more, and on heavily worked streams, the water may be worthless until the next day.

Rising To The Occasion

The trout is lying behind a rock at a depth of 3 feet. The slower the drift the more time the fish has to examine the fly as the fish rises to the surface. Where you see a trout rise and take food is usually several feet downstream from his lie because of the drift. Therefore, the angler must cast ahead of the riseform where the fish touches the surface.

By coming up on the fish from downstream, you can work each section of the pool carefully, pulling a trout out of each holding area, playing it firmly (but not horsing it to you) without scaring off other fish. With luck the other trout will not have seen the action and the current will cover a good portion of the sound of the struggle.

Some of the largest fish in a stream will hold in the tail of a pool, in the smooth water, just before it drops over falls or breaks in a rapidly-moving riffle. The advantages of feeding here are that the food is concentrated as the channel frequently narrows and that the water is shallow enough to allow the fish an excellent view both in the water and to some degree above.

An angler willing to crouch down and make a careful approach has an advantage because the water is not deep, and thus the fish's field of vision is restricted (remember—the deeper the trout holds, the wider its field of vision). To heighten your advantage, fish these locations during overcast days or in the early mornings and evenings during periods of low light when the trout are less cautious. Another advantage for the savvy angler is that most anglers pass this water over in favor of the better-looking, deeper water at the head of the pool. Less angling pressure equals more undisturbed fish.

On small streams, you can often cast up into this water by standing below the tail in the stream. If you see any fish working either on the surface or along the bottom, try to cast several feet above them and at a slight angle so that your line does not cover the trout and scare them. Work from one side to the other in an orderly fashion to get as much mileage from the location as possible.

This also holds true on big rivers, but you will often be casting long distances from shore or well above you from an anchored boat. On really big water, look for slower currents—the flat-looking water right next to the choppy, broken stuff. Trout hold right along the edge.

Side Eddies Deliver The Goods

Those swirling, revolving pieces of water that form on either or both sides of a pool are natural delivery troughs for trout. Any food source that is not caught in the main current as it travels through the pool, winds up drifting around and around in an eddy.

Trout will rest just inside of this current, in the eye of the flow where very little energy is needed to maintain position. Fish just along the edge of the broken water on the edge of the slower water. Often, a foam line or pile of foam with a swirling vortex marks the middle where food concentrates. Working the lines of foam or allowing the lure, bait or fly to swirl around in the foam eddy will take very big fish.

When these eddies form along gravel and sand bottoms, deposits of drifting debris will form a bank or shallow shelf near shore. Trout will hold in the deeper water away from shore in such spots. Often, the fish will be facing downstream, but still facing into the current that has reversed itself in the swirl. This phenomenon must be taken into account when approaching the

How Trout Use The Bottom For Shelter

Trout are deployed in classic holding lies in this drawing. The calmer bottom or bethnic currents are places of shelter (A) that hold the most fish. Smaller and similar spots (B, C and D) in other parts of the pond also are places to look for holding trout.

trout. If you can guess their position, you can sneak into casting range without spooking them.

When these eddies churn against a loose rock or earthen bank, fish will hold along the loose-rock ledge created by the erosive qualities of the swirl or back beneath the undercut earthen bank. Undercut banks are always hideouts for trout, but tough to fish because slipping an offering beneath them is next to impossible with straight, downstream current. Fortunately, in the case of an eddy, the spinning water will carry the lure directly to the fish, making the presentation relatively simple.

Middle Portion Holds Plenty Of Fish

In an ideal pool, if there is such a thing, the main current runs through the center, or middle part of the pool. This area is

Double Fly Rig

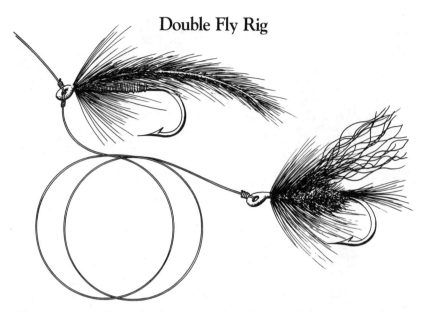

The easiest way to fish two dry flies, or a dry fly and a nymph, is to tie an extra length of monofilament right to the eye of the first fly. This double fly rig, or "New Zealand tie," is not only quick, with no changes in the original leader, but the two patterns seldom tangle.

often defined by a standing wave that resembles a ridge. During periods of high or normal flow, this area is too fast for trout to hold in, but they will be found on either side of the wave waiting for anything edible to drift past. Whether you are fishing a small creek or a large river, this faster seam is easily spotted by the standing wave or, at least, a rough line of so-called broken water.

No matter what size water being fished, during normal flows trout will not be found in the main current but on the sides. In large pools this may be many yards away, or the distance needed to find calmer water. Most times of the day and throughout the year, fishing down deep in the calmer benthic currents will produce more fish. Trout are not often found holding in the middle portions of the water column. They will either be down deep or, less frequently, on top feeding on emerging insects. The middle section is mainly a travel corridor.

Between the times when water levels drop in mid-summer and they rise again in the spring, this main current stem may be the only spot in the pool that has sufficient flow to provide cool, oxygenated water, shelter and adequate food delivery. So, instead of working the sides as you would early in the year, fish right down the gut of the pool drifting your bait or lure down along the bottom. When trout are visible feeding at or near the surface, use a dry fly, nymph or small spinner or spoon.

Look For Shelves At Heads Of Pools

Whenever a stream narrows and shoots over a shelf and into a pool, the darker, deeper water will hold trout, often very large ones. The reason is that just over this lip is an almost dead calm piece of water that allows a fish to hold easily and still snatch any food drifting by overhead. Cast up on the shelf well above this spot and allow the bait to drift down into the hole.

This will often take several casts. Do not be discouraged if the first attempt fails to turn a fish. If the offering does not pass directly over a trout or very near it, nothing will happen. When the cast is right, the fish will take. These holding areas are not large, and trout do not have a lot of room to work in, making them opportunistic feeders.

Sometimes the current enters the pool in the form of a plunge pool, easily detected because of the "cloud" of white, bubbling, well-oxygenated water. Rarely will trout hold at the head or in the middle of this bubbling spot. The currents swirling in a multitude of directions are just too strong and complicated to offer efficient feeding. The fish will once again be along the sides or at the end of the cloud. Casts along the sides or into the middle and working toward the end of this water will attract the trout's attention.

An exception in plunge pools can sometimes be found at the head of the pool where the water looks the most severe. The gouging action of the current rushing down from the above run sometimes digs out an undercut that is calm enough to hold trout that lie in wait for any food source that rolls up in front of them. Getting an offering into a trout's view here is difficult. Casting across stream rarely puts a lure in the right spot. And neither does casting upstream. Many casts and patience are required to obtain that one perfect drift and catch.

Tailwaters Are Big Trout Locations

Tailwaters—those immense, cool flows of water below large dams—are some of the hottest fishing-for-trophy trout found

The quick-plunging falls found on smaller streams create pools that are ideal places for many of the larger trout to hang out.

anywhere. Because there is strong current and the water is often pulled from the cold depths of the reservoir above, ideal trout habitat is created. Also, fish are sucked through from the lake above and chewed up by the power-generating turbines, creating a constant "chum" that monster trout gorge on. Also, good levels of nutrients are delivered from the water system behind the dam, which creates luxuriant plant growth for a variety of aquatic insects.

Bait drifted along the bottom directly below these dams will take these trout better than any other method. Because waters such as those found on dams below the Columbia or Missouri rivers are often huge, NAFC members will find heavy tackle, a lot of weight and a big bait (like a large minnow) will work best in attracting fish that have a lot to choose from. As always, work any apparent calmer edges that seam next to faster water.

Once these hefty flows smooth out and calm down, often hundreds of yards downstream, the habitat is the same as that commonly found in most trout streams, though very fertile and extremely productive in nature.

Dams produce excellent tailwater trout fisheries in areas that were formerly devoid of fish, or marginal at best. A world-class example is the Bighorn River below Yellowtail Dam. This is one of the best rivers anywhere for big browns and rainbows. Before the dam was built, this was lousy water more suited to suckers. Unfortunately, tailwaters are so good that they become extremely crowded, producing less than ideal angling conditions. The first few years that a water like this opens up, before "the word gets out," are the prime time to fish.

=18=

Riffles And Runs

On most trout streams, a lot more mileage is racked up by riffles and runs than by pools. Riffles and runs are those long, fast-moving stretches of water that connect pools. They are frequently excellent locations for catching lots of trout, some of which will be big boys. Riffles and runs are also frequently overlooked by many anglers, which is an added bonus for those anglers who are familiar with their excellent qualities. The fewer people fishing any water, the better it will be.

Simply put, a run is a stretch of water on a river or stream that takes water to a lower elevation. When this flow is sufficiently shallow—from a couple of inches to perhaps 4 feet—where any disturbance along a gravel or small rock bottom is displayed on the surface, the run is a riffle. You know, those choppy-looking, bouncy stretches of a stream that you never fish.

Because most of the best runs are deep and dark, and because many of the choice riffles are shallow and somewhat transparent in nature, anglers have a tendency to assume that they hold few if any trout and the few that might be found in these environments will probably be small.

Such is hardly the case. Many of the true "hogs" of any stream are found at one time or another in these two types of water. And a very big plus for NAFC members is the fact that both are relatively straightforward to fish. For the most part, the

Fishing a cast all the way through from its upstream beginnings downstream is a good approach to taking trout. However, wading and working downstream comes in a poor second.

Riffles And Runs

need for an extreme amount of weight, pinpoint casting and interpretation of layer upon layer of flickering current is basically nonexistent.

Plenty Of Food Tumbles Down Riffles

Riffles are one of the most productive areas of a river for aquatic insects. The shallowness of the water allows plenty of sunlight to reach the bottom, sparking rapid and lush algae growth for the bugs to feed upon. Nymphs will be crawling all over the bottom—along the gravels, up and over rocks, down in the tiny spaces between gravels and rocks.

Trout move up out of their safe, deep-water holding areas to feed on these and occasionally on forage fish that are zipping about doing the same thing.

In truly shallow riffles of less than 18 inches, fly fishing is by far the most productive method. Spinners pull to the surface and spoons clank clumsily along the bottom. Bait cast upstream and rolled and bounced along the gravels has many of the attributes of a nymph or emerger worked in this water, but flies are more easily controlled because the angler can mend his thicker and heavier fly line up or downstream as conditions dictate. The secret on these stretches of water is to obtain as natural a drift as possible, which usually means having the nymph bouncing along and among the gravels and rocks where the trout are nosing about. Weight is rarely required in this shallow water. Leaders of 9 feet and more help the angler approach the trout with stealth.

Tailers Provide Serious Sport

In shallow riffles and even shallower flats (slow, smooth water) trout will be seen "tailing." This is when they are grubbing along the bottom feeding on nymphs and their tails are visible breaking the surface. Because they are working in such shallow water, they have almost no window of vision (physics again) and are, therefore, unable to effectively identify food passing overhead. Yet, due to the richness of insect life in this kind of water, trout come into these shallows to feed along the bottoms on the myriads of nymphs—especially during the heat of the day when bug activity is peaking. At midday, the logical play would seem to be the deep, dark pools, but the

One of the secrets to taking trout in riffles and runs is to work the seams of the current such as the seam indicated in the lefthand portion of this picture.

riffles are a productive paradox from an angler's perspective.

Spotting a fish and then casting well above and slightly across (again to avoid line spooking) and then carefully drifting the nymph down to the trout takes skill and produces many fish over 20 inches in ankle-deep water. Fighting such a trout in this shallowness is exhilarating.

Upstream is the preferred approach since trout are extremely jittery in this water because it leaves them wide open to predation from above.

In slightly deeper riffles, a streamer cast up and across stream and then stripped in quick darts and flashes will trigger slashing responses from larger trout who think they have hammered an unsuspecting minnow.

The same is also true for a spinner tossed directly upstream or slightly across current and worked back just quickly enough to impart action to the blade, a tactic that will take plenty of trout. Line tension between reel and the lure is required as is a constant adjustment of retrieval speed to match the varying current speeds. The same approach with bait will work and bouncing it easily along the bottom can also turn trout successfully. Nymphs, worms and hoppers on the surface, especially near grassy banks, work the best.

A couple of other points to remember regarding riffles are that when fishing wide-open stretches, look for any depression or hole in the streambed, no matter how small. Darker patches in the water indicate these locations. When trout are present in shallow riffles, many times the biggest fish will hold in these tiny pockets of cover waiting, somewhat secure from predators, for any passing morsel. When a riffle flows past brushy or tree-lined banks, work the water closest to shore—hard. This is an ideal location for trout. It's one location where trout can dart safely to and from cover while making feeding runs out in the open.

And, when an entire stretch of river is one big riffle, look for anything that offers cover, or fish the riffle where it begins to smooth out and slow down a touch. This is better territory than the faster, rough water above.

Flats Are A Transition Zone

Flats are those lazy, dead flat, seemingly lifeless transition zones between riffles and runs or pools, but there are times when they can hold plenty of trout.

When insects hatch here in abundance, or when forage fish are out eating smaller bugs like midge pupae, older fish, especially big browns slice up from their undercut banks or deep-water holding spots in the evening and cruise these flats looking for big bites.

Trout are fuel efficient, so working flats often provides the fish plenty of calories without expending much energy. The main difference here is that instead of looking for the slower water like you do in a riffle, you are searching for any increase in current, no matter how slight, that will move a greater concentration of food in a shorter time to the fish.

Minnows and smaller trout also are attracted to these areas

Spinners used in this riffle of the Cascade River in Canada's Banff National Park produced large trout, even in daylight. A quartering cast upstream permits tension to spin the blade.

and trout of 5 pounds or more have no problem whatsoever dining graciously on pan-sized trout. How do you think browns started being called cannibals?

Trout Stack Up In Runs

Some of the best fishing for really large trout is in deep runs, water over 4 feet, and often coursing downstream in a narrow chute. On big flows, the entire river from bank to bank can be a run and sometimes this occurs on smaller streams when the channel narrows such as when a creek squeezes through a steep-walled canyon.

There are good runs that are no more than 4 feet deep, 10 feet wide and maybe 100 feet long. These wild places have yielded trout over 10 pounds.

Your first reaction might be that nothing will be taken from this raging run. However, trout will hold in the calmer water on either side of the run, so work those areas.

Most of the time the best fish in these runs will be holding down deep behind a rock or boulder or in a slight depression in the streambed—anywhere the current is blocked or slowed down. Any bait, lure or fly drifted down along the bottom will take these fish that are opportunistic feeders. Any kind of food source washed through their feeding lane and right above their heads will be taken quickly, which is an advantage for the angler. The fish are not always as selective as their pool-dwelling counterparts.

Work All The Way Through The Bottom Of A Run

With heavy nymphs and streamers connected to short, stout leaders (like 3 or 4 feet with 1X tippet) and most lures, no additional weight is required if the cast is made almost directly

Loop-Knot

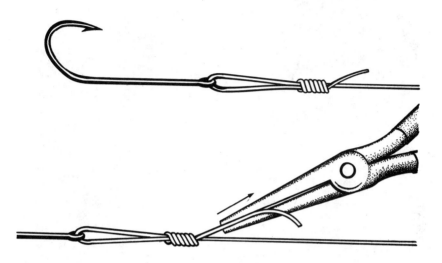

The loop knot is a uni-knot (see page 247) that is pulled tight, as shown, short of the hook eye. It's a good choice for giving more action to the lure when fishing stream bottoms.

upstream in the run. By the time the lure is even with you on a 40-foot cast with a fly rod it will be working well down along the bottom. Fish the cast all the way through and let it swing out and hang in the current for several seconds at the finish. Often a large fish has drifted back beneath, watching the fly, and will take just on this swing or even when it is dangling in the current. Takes at this time are sharp and often result in broken leaders. Setting the hook is not as easy, either, because you are pulling upstream and away from the fish.

All of this holds true for spinning (and bait when sufficient weight is applied so it reaches the proper depth). The difference with lures is that you will be fishing the bottom much sooner and because you will be throwing longer casts, you will be trying to control line at a greater distance. This will require a rapid retrieve when the lure is upstream of your position. You want the line to be tight and the lure moving quickly enough to have action and you only need a little of this in this fast water, just enough to catch a trout's eye. Spinners and spoons are perfect for this fishing.

Once the line is below you, you may have to release the

Trout fishermen will recognize this as a classic riffle that forms at the tail of a pool. Trout will hold in this water, feeding on insects, nymphs and small minnows that gather there.

Complete Anglers Library

spool and let out line, controlling the tension with your fingers. When a fish takes at these times, letting go of the line and clicking the bail closed, all in one brief, smooth motion will plant the hook, although certain elements of luck are involved, but then so does luck permeate most fishing.

On Big Rivers Drift The Runs

On really large rivers that you fish from a boat, one of the best methods is to drift down along the outside edge of a run and cast upstream toward shore, working the line the same way you would if you were fishing from shore or while wading.

The main difference here is that you will be moving at approximately the same speed as the current so you will get a much longer drift, and in the process, fish the line you are working more effectively. The disadvantage is that you will only have one opportunity to fish a stretch of water unless you move back upstream and work it again. Eventually the boat will scare off the trout.

Whenever NAFC members are in doubt about where to begin fishing runs (or any other water for that matter) on large rivers, they should work the slicks along the banks. Because of the shelter offered by bankside obstructions such as downed trees and boulders in the shallower water, there will be more opportunities for trout to find calm water for resting. Start near shore and gradually work your way out into the big water of the main run.

Finally, always remember that trout are fish of the seams, no matter how large or small the water you are fishing. Wherever there is a seam—a dividing line between fast and slow water, there will be fish holding in slow water right on the edge of the fast stuff. Foam lines (lines of bubbles on the water), smooth, slick water next to rough flows—these are the indications of seams in a river and they mean good fishing.

19

Banks

The most logical place to look for trout on a stream is along the banks, and with good reason. There is shelter here. Often the most productive current threads run next to the bank and all sorts of insects fall into the water from the grasses, bushes and trees nearby. Cool springs often seep into a river from its banks.

If you are fishing unfamiliar water, you could do much worse than beginning to fish the banks with determination.

Some of the main types of bank structure include undercuts, riprap, cutbanks, brush- or tree-lined, grassy and rocky. Each has its share of fish, some more than others.

One general rule supersedes all others when bank fishing—when a line of foam or bubbles are visible, fish your lure, bait or fly in the line first, no matter how the rest of the water looks. Trout key on these prime food delivery lanes.

One other generality is to always fish the water directly below the entrance of a stream or spring. This cold, oxygenated water is loaded with insects, nutrients, and many times, forage fish. The deeper water is clearly visible as a darker shelf where the flow pours in or as a dark pocket tucked into the bank just below the creek.

Undercuts Are Big-Time Shelter
Undercut banks, even those little-lipped ones of 6 inches, are one of the best locations for big trout in any stream. No

This brushy bank will hold many fine trout but whatever method an angler chooses, he must work it right into the tangles in order to take fish. Cast quartering upstream, bank tight.

Banks

matter how big a fish grows, the most serious threats to its life from predation come from above in the form of birds, like eagles and ospreys, or animals such as minks, martins and raccoons, to name a few. Undercuts provide shelter and by their very nature, a steady delivery of food.

When a river's current swings tight against an earthen bank or water rushes head-long into the same location after being deflected by some object such as a bridge piling or boulder or shift in course, the erosion of the soil creates den-like structures of darkness and protection, often beneath a tangle of roots. Many undercut banks go back several feet, but even a very big trout is only a few inches wide, so a half foot of cover will give all the room it needs.

No matter what method NAFC members are using, getting the offering underneath to where the trout is holding is critical. Big fish will not move far from their holes. They don't need to move because the current brings the food right to their mouths.

Often casting dead straight across stream and allowing the flow to carry the lure under the bank works well, particularly with bait. Another method is to cast tight to the bank from downstream and work the bait or lure back to you, always maintaining tension or contact with the line. Flies and lures retrieved this way, especially brightly colored, flashy items that snap any available light back underneath the bank to catch a trout's eye, will turn fish.

You will lose gear if you are fishing this water properly, so use heavier line. If you normally use 4-pound test, step up to 6 or even 8. If your tippet size is usually 3X or 4X, move up to 1X or 0X. Big fish in these swift-water, darkened conditions are not leader-shy.

Riprap Is Deceiving

Riprap, that ugly jumble of rocks or concrete piled along stream banks to prevent erosion, often holds some nice trout.

The best way to fish this structure is from a boat and casting into it, working any hole or drop-off much as you would pocket water. Much of the riprap you pass will be barren, while another section that is almost identical to the fishless ones will hold bunches of trout. In these cases, even the fisheries biologists are stumped. Trout have their whims and behavior

Working streamers tight to undercut and overgrown banks produces nice brown trout like this 22-incher that took a sculpin.

anomalies like the rest of us.

Because the current is usually strong in these places (if it were not, there would not be any riprap in the first place), bait fishing is tough unless you use a car bumper for a sinker. Heavy spinners, weighted minnows, spoons and weighted streamers and nymphs work well. Often with flies, you will need to use some lead attached a foot or so above the pattern and, in some extreme cases, a sink-tip line in order to drop the offering down to the fish.

Cutbanks Attract Big Fish

Cutbanks can be excellent locations to work for big fish. Gravel banks are always collapsing into the stream producing new, clean gravels that large trout love come spawning time.

Any method will take fish in these spots as long as whatever is used is cast far upstream and carefully worked along the bottom where the trout are holding. One truly effective method is to quarter a cast upstream with a red-and-white spoon, allow it to sink to the bottom and then work it with just a touch of flutter, dancing the lure almost straight-up with the hook-end teasing the bottom. Trout cannot resist this, hitting the lure with an upward strike and often, in the shallower runs, rolling on the surface like a musky.

Clay banks break off in chunks and sheets that slide and drop into a river leaving mini-streams, flows and pockets between them and the main banks.

Slipping a spinner or attractive little streamer in these spots is tough but worth the effort. After a week or two in the water, the compressed soil will have been gouged by the current resulting in trout-sized pockets, designer housing as it were. These pockets are *never* fished and when an offering zips by, the trout will take. Trout seem to be gullible to an angler's deceptive nature in these locations because they are safe from many of their predators.

Brushy Or Tree-lined Banks Are Hard To Beat

If you have been stream-fishing for trout more than five minutes, you know to fish brushy or tree-lined banks. These locations always hold trout. The limbs and branches provide shelter from airborne predators and contribute a ready supply of insects to the trout holding below. The roots of this growth hold banks together for a couple of feet in depth, creating the previously-discussed undercut situations.

You fish this habitat dead-tight and upstream with whatever you have. The only changes here are if you see fish work at or near the surface. Then, you must try to match the hatch to some extent if you are fishing flies. But spinner and baitfishers can proceed about their business as usual. A spinner or minnow zipped through feeding trout will do one of two things—scare the hell out of them and put them off their feed or provoke violent strikes from fish that are already at a fever pitch from the current-feeding activity.

The same holds true with a fly fisher using streamers. Slip or slide, two casts will tell the story. The trout will either have

Casting tight to bankside obstructions such as these rocks protruding into the current normally takes trout that will hold behind each obstruction or in each pocket.

"gone south" or be so far into a feeding frenzy that they will hit anything, admittedly an uncommon occurrence, but fabulous fishing when it flashes briefly across an angler's horizon. *Avoid* areas where a tree limb or other similar object projects out several feet above the water. These are ideal perches for fish-eating birds, causing trout to stay away from these areas.

Grassy Banks And Terrestrials

Bunches of green grasses waving in a warm afternoon breeze next to a trout stream are a sure sign of prime fishing. Grasshoppers, beetles, crickets, ants—you name it—wind up in the nearby water.

Ask any experienced trout fisher to name a half dozen or so of his best times on the water and chances are one of them will be fishing terrestrials, usually hoppers, on a warm, summer day.

These creatures are large chunks of protein that are either present in good numbers or not around much at all. They are easy for a trout to see and easy to take, being basically helpless once trapped on the surface film. When you are really in luck and are fishing near, say, a hay field that a farmer is harvesting,

When making fine, difficult casts to the bank, a tight loop in the fly line maintains the energy of the cast and the accuracy. How does an angler throw one of these consistently? Watch an expert and then practice, practice, practice.

hoppers will be flying everywhere and so will the trout. Once the bugs start dropping on the water, trout will key on them and feed steadily throughout the day. Most of this fishing takes place after mid-morning when the sun has been up long enough to warm the air and get the insects moving.

Fly fishers casting upstream, bank-tight from out in the river with an adequate imitation of what is plopping on the water, often take big fish on every cast in good runs. The same is true for baitfishers.

Another way to fish these banks is to extend your rod with a tight line out over the water right next to the bank, working the hopper, cricket or other terrestrial as you walk very quietly and as far back as possible from the bank. Dapping, as this deadly technique is called, will produce savage strikes and is one of the best big-fish methods around. Heavier-than-normal line or leaders are required because the savage strikes leave little room for error. You will be playing the trout right off the tip of the rod. So, leave that classy cane rod or delicate ultra-light spinning rod at home. A little stouter stuff is needed here.

Also, grasses often grow so thick that they create a tunnel over the water that is in many ways like an undercut bank. Banging a fly or lure through the growth and working through this tunnel turns up trout.

Finally, terrestrials are not confined to grassy banks. NAFC members should be alert to terrestrial activity along any type of bank. The feeding excitement these insects create provides some of the finest trout fishing there is.

20

Fixed Objects In Current

Trout take advantage of every opportunity for food and shelter that any water system offers them. Fixed objects in the middle of streams and rivers are classic examples. Minute depressions in a streambed caused by current swirling around a midstream rock in a stream in Colorado, protection from predation afforded by strands of barbed wire through or over a meadow creek in Michigan, remnants of an old covered bridge splitting the current of a Pennsylvania spring creek—these are but a few examples of the kinds of objects trout will use.

While trout often keep to bankside or deep-water holding areas during bright daylight, fish that take up residence around fixed objects tend to behave differently. Any bit of food floating by is worthy of examination and possible consumption by these fish, no matter what time of the day.

The Ever-Popular Midstream Boulder

The most obvious fixed object found in current is usually a boulder or large rock located in the middle of a strong tongue of current. Water racing around both sides often shows a broken, whitewater surface. A smooth, glassy slick stretches downstream in a gradually diminishing cone shape. Even people who do not fish will stop and examine this type of water, looking for something. Perhaps, it's remnants of the hunter in all of us and this type of water triggers an atavistic, or throw back response.

This weedbed in the middle of the current holds trout right at its edges that can be taken by thoroughly working the edges.

Fixed Objects In Current

The reasons are not important here. What is, is the fact that this type of habitat is some of the most consistent on a trout stream. No matter how many miles of choice brushy, undercut banks or how many deep pools a river may have, midstream boulders will have their share of trout, many of them among the largest to be found.

A classic example of this is the Madison River flowing between Earthquake Lake and Ennis Lake in southwestern Montana. Often referred to as a "50-mile riffle," this water is littered with boulders varying in size from that of a 26-inch television set to a small house. Every year thousands of browns and rainbows of 20 inches or more are taken by anglers fishing from shore, whether they are wading or working from Mackenzie River drift boats.

Another good example is the Brule River in northwestern Wisconsin. This stream has every kind of big trout water imaginable, but, once again, a large percentage of the best trout caught each season come from around boulders. The same is true for the smaller mountain streams in the Smoky Mountains, the Housatonic, the Connecticut and countless others. Few experienced anglers will pass up the opportunity to toss at least a cast or two to these objects when working a river, no matter how good the rest of the holding water is.

Fish Down Instead Of Up

Midstream boulders are a very big exception to the advice you've heard about always fishing upstream. The reason is relatively straightforward, in a circular sort of way.

In strong currents, you can take good fish by first working the front of the rock, where there is a sizable depression carved out by water action. (By probing with a stick on the upstream side of a rock in a milder run, you can see how deep the depression runs beneath the rock.) Cast upstream to allow your lure to work down on the bottom and then over the lip into this type of hole. The take will be swift, and you will have to lift the rod to guide the trout out into the open.

Next work the near side and then the far side of the rock, allowing the offering to swing back around the rock. There are usually a couple of trout holding in the calm area right behind the boulder downstream. Then launch a cast or two into the

Casting above midstream obstructions such as this partial dam is a good place to find holding trout. They may be small trout but they will be trout all the same.

water directly behind the rock, allowing time for the bait to sink near the bottom before retrieving it quickly across stream.

Finally, cast downstream below where the smooth water ends and the roily, choppy current resumes. Retrieve upstream back through the slick. Many times the best fish of the hole will strike within a couple of feet (or even inches) of the spot where the lure or fly entered the smooth water. This occurs because the current spins around and past the boulder creating an eddy that reverses the flow of water bringing food back upstream. Fish face downstream to take advantage of this protein merry-go-round.

So, by fishing downstream you may lose a fish or two in the first piece of water, but you will preserve your chances for taking what is frequently the best fish in the pocket.

Ledges Obstruct Current And Hold Trout

Rock ledges, strictly speaking, are not midstream objects, but wherever a ledge or wall of rock juts out into the current at even a slight angle creating a small pool and a place of calm, no matter how tiny, there will be trout.

In raging canyon rivers, these locations can hold huge trout that are rarely fished and, because of the strength of the current, these fish must take quick advantage of every food source that roars past.

Reaching this water productively with bait is almost impossible and only slightly less difficult with spinning gear or flies. Casts well across stream and far upstream are required and then effective drift is only a few feet, sometimes lasting less than a second. Many casts are required to fish these places of isolation and turbulence, but they are worth the effort.

If a trout does hit, getting it across the current to you is another story. Heavy-duty gear is required to handle the water and the fish. Medium-weight or heavier spinning gear or at least 7-weight and larger fly rods are a must. This is not easy fishing.

Trees, Logs And Fences

Fishing midstream objects is similar in most cases with the exceptions of trees. Currents swirl in the same way around trees, logs and fences as they do around boulders, but trees often have limbs sticking down into the water hiding trout. Casting into this is costly in lost tackle. Fish around trees in current by first working from downstream up to the tree and then work your way quietly to the upstream side and fish down. Little holding water will be wasted this way.

Unfortunately, getting your lure well back into a tree or log lying perpendicular to a stream flow is the only way to fish it properly. First, cast up close to the object, as much to gauge distance as to take fish, which you may well do. Then, gradually work your way inward until you start getting hung up consistently or lose your patience (this may very well be a simultaneous occurrence).

Sweepers are limbs of trees both living and dead that lay in or just above the water parallel to the surface and they should always be fished in the same way that you fish the above objects. Always fish any foam line or bubble line railing off the

Brown trout are considered by many anglers to be the toughest trout to catch. This logjam "dam" has created a spot where the angler, using proper stealth, can find them.

tip of these objects. Good trout tend to stack up along these threads of productive current.

When any of these objects are lying parallel to the bank, fish from downstream casting up alongside of the log or tree, as close as possible. Trout will be stacked the length of this water, both just along the object and beneath it. Cutthroats, in particular, love this type of structure.

Logjams Are Tangles Of Trout

Massive piles of dead trees and limbs and other accumulated debris are trout hotels. There are swirls, eddies, pools and other areas of dead calm that will never, ever see anything cast by an angler. Some of these jams are 50 feet wide and over 100 feet long. Biologists who have snorkled such monstrosities report

Fixed Objects In Current   219 being scared out of their wits when working up close to a submerged tangle and suddenly seeing a head the size of a small log, mouth open and full of teeth, of course, poking out to see who is visiting.

Because these types of cover have such potential, working a lure, bait or streamer down into them from upstream or even directly above by crawling over the jam is worthwhile. You may never hook a fish and if you do, you may never derrick it out of its hole, but life is a crapshoot anyway, so give these a try.

Remember to be extremely careful around this area. If you slip and are washed into the jam, you're a goner. If you fall through, the least you can expect is a badly sprained ankle. Caution, always caution, is the operative word when on, in or near moving water. It is amazing how fast so many bad things can happen once an angler loses his footing in a river.

Man-Made Objects Draw Trout

The objects of mankind's "creative" endeavors influencing trout behavior can range from bridge pilings to fence posts to wooden cribs and deflectors to abandoned Volvos. All of these objects attract trout. They provide shelter from predators and the current. Smaller fish and aquatic insects are found near them, too.

Bridges, especially when they are close to the water's surface, draw trout like magnets. The illusion of safety from predators is created and the pilings and other related structure break up the current and provide habitat in a fashion almost identical to that of midstream boulders. The only difference, and it is a major one, is that fishing upstream is more productive, especially for the fly fisher.

Often trout rise steadily to insects hatching just upstream from the bridge in the sunlight, plucking them from the surface as they drift through the shade. Flies cast upstream in such places are deadly. The odd fish facing downstream to catch the upstream flow is worth spooking for an opportunity to take greater numbers of trout feeding in the open.

Many small bridges and crossings have culverts passing the water beneath them. The shooting water on the downstream side digs out a large basin and trout hold on either side and back underneath the plunging water. Streamers worked across this

Trolling "cowbells" and a small spoon in deep water produces trout like this rainbow. For some reason, bells and whistles seem to work in attracting trout at that depth.

water perpendicular to the current are particularly effective. Bait allowed to work around in the water is next on the list.

Wood Cribs And Deflectors Have Their Places

Oftentimes, a stream has been severely damaged by channelization, nearby development, clear-cutting of its riparian areas or overgrazing by livestock. When this happens on a formerly great trout stream, area anglers often join with local fisheries departments to reconstruct the habitat. These efforts often take the form of wooden cribs lashed to the bank to provide cover, log or stone spill dams to create pools and flush away sediments and deflectors that also flush sediments and re-aim current in more productive directions.

Once a trout population begins to re-establish itself, the fish will be found along and under the wooden cribs. Food is delivered directly to the trout while they hold securely beneath the structure. These are great spots for trout, but they're tough to fish with flies unless a large hatch draws out the trout.

The flash of spinners and spoons will draw the fish. Bait, like worms or larvae, worked very slowly but with some motion

Fixed Objects In Current

As a construction object, this bridge channels food sources and provides overhead protection, making it a good bet for picking up trout.

along the bottom will take trout.

Construction that creates pools is not that tough to fish. You work the water using the same methods discussed in Chapter 17 on pools. During the first years, the water will not be as deep and the pool will not be clearly defined, meaning fewer and smaller trout that may be scattered anywhere in the water. As time passes and more and more material is scoured away and the hole deepens, the standard pool structure asserts itself and typical trout fishing resurfaces.

Deflectors create trout habitat, but not right along the structures themselves. Fish the seams and lines of foam and bubbles downstream from the ends of these objects. The trout will be holding here, much as they would below a downed tree or a sweeper.

They Really Do Use Cars

Rarely will you find cars embedded in the middle of a trout stream, although they are occasionally spotted protruding out into the current, having shifted from their bank-holding position with the passage of time and water.

These poor things rusting away silently beneath an unforgiving sun do hold trout, but catching such a beautiful fish next to a fading chartreuse Edsel seems to lack a certain degree of aesthetic charm.

Lakes And
Reservoirs

21

Surface Fishing On Lakes

I n many respects, fishing for trout on lakes and reservoirs is
some of the most rewarding angling around. When you
find the trout, whether they are actively feeding on or
near the surface or you are taking them down deep, you
usually bump into a bunch of them.

Then, there are those days of famine, when even on smaller
lakes the fish seem impossible to locate. An angler begins to
think he has been cast adrift on a liquid desert and in some ways
he has. Even in the most fertile and productive trout waters,
the amount of volume or biomass that trout contribute to the
overall picture is minuscule, next to nothing.

So when an angler approaches fishing a lake or reservoir,
the image of a vast desert is not that far off target. Most of the
time most of the water is fishless. There may not be a trout for
many miles in large bodies of water. As was seen in Chapter 10,
there are ways to narrow down the water to be searched, things
to look for. But what do you do once you find the trout? Flailing
away at the water will drive the trout away. A rational approach
is called for.

As with any type of fishing, preparation, observation and
attention to detail reap dividends. This applies to catching
trout on lakes and reservoirs on the surface, in subsurface
fishing, along shorelines and around river mouths, and in the
frigid depths of winter when you are fleeing the dreaded malady,
"cabin fever," by seeking trout through the ice.

This is what you are after—really nice trout. This NAFC member took a pair of Lahotan cutthroat trout from Pyramid Lake, Nevada.

Surface Fishing On Lakes 227

Effectively fishing the surface water of lakes and reservoirs involves one of the main ingredients of successful stream angling—stealth. A less than careful approach will spook trout in a hurry.

When trout take an insect on the surface, then quickly drop back down in the water, they accomplish a couple of things. The first is that their window of vision is expanded. Secondly, they protect themselves from aerial attacks from predators such as fish hawks or osprey. Prime examples of this behavior are grayling that rise up from a lake bottom through many feet of water to take in an insect, and then just as quickly dart right back down to safety.

Exceptions, Always Exceptions

The exceptions to this, holding special importance to the angler, are when clusters of insects are bouncing about the surface or trapped in the surface film. Then, trout will move quickly from one bug to the next, slurping in a bunch of protein with very little expenditure of energy.

Catching actively feeding fish on the surface is the true province of the fly fisher. Working from shore or casting from a float tube, canoe or other craft, anyone who can cast 35 to 40 feet with reasonable accuracy (meaning hitting an imaginary 3-foot circle) without stirring up the water will consistently catch trout.

From a stealth standpoint, float tubes are ideal because they have such a low profile on the water. You are right on the surface, with just your head and part of your chest above water. The part of your body below the surface does not seem to scare the trout. In fact, many times a hooked fish will run straight for your legs thinking that protective cover is near. This can create some interesting maneuvers on the part of both the angler and the fish.

Because trout become so tuned to rapid feeding at times of aquatic insect abundance, as soon as a trout rises normally making the classic "dimpled" or circular rise-form, the angler should shoot a cast to the exact same spot. The slight disturbance of the fly hitting the water should catch a fish's attention and provoke an immediate response. If not, twitch the fly slightly.

Trout's Cone Of Vision

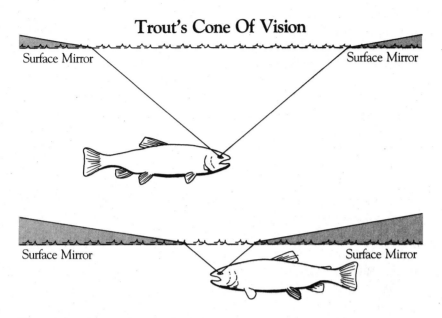

This is the trout's cone of vision. The angle at the vertex remains constant so that when the trout is nearer the surface, the window is smaller. However, the trout sees everything within the window so an angler needs to avoid the "window" in approaching likely trout locations.

If fish refuse to take after several casts, change flies and try for a closer match to what is hatching on the water. There will be spinners, discarded nymph cases and emerging insects all around you for reference.

If, after switching to a natural fly pattern, you still fail to turn fish, lengthen your leader by attaching a tippet section of 2 feet or more in the next size smaller than you were currently using. In some conditions, you may want to be fishing 15 feet or more of leader in 4X or smaller when you encounter leader-shy trout or extremely bright light and clear water.

A good deal of sound and fury is expended in "serious" angling circles stating that tippets should never exceed 18 to 24 inches because anything longer will not allow a fly to turn over at the end of a cast properly. How a fly turns over runs an extremely poor second to "lining" the fish. Putting the fly on the water without stampeding the trout is the prime objective. If size, shape and color (in that order of importance) are matched, and the pattern hits the surface without spooking the trout, most of the time things will run their productive, fish-catching course.

Dropping down to smaller and smaller tippets is a trade-off situation, especially when casting to good fish. What you gain in increased takes is offset to some degree by break-offs due to weaker line strength. Most anglers prefer increased action over fishing secure in the knowledge that they will not lose the few trout they do take.

Lifting Nymphs To Surface Is Deadly

A killer method for taking trout that are working the surface is to fish a weighted nymph a couple of feet below the surface and then slowly bring it up, or *lift* it, to the surface. This mimics the behavior of the natural as it struggles to the top before it rises into the air. Strikes from trout keyed into this behavior are savage and many large trout concentrate their efforts on this just-below-the-surface action rather than working the surface.

When damselflies are present in a lake, especially when they are buzzing around in the air in good numbers, either a Sheep Creek or Prince Nymph works wonders. Both are olive green and look like the damselfly nymph. When these bugs are active and you fail to take trout on either pattern, go home and read about fishing. It's not your day.

Dry-fly imitations of damselflies are beautiful to look at, and there are times when they will take trout after trout after trout. Compared to the productivity of the nymphal imitations, though, their significance to the angler pales.

This lift method works with most nymphs including Hare's Ears, which are something of a universal pattern that take trout in almost any water, anywhere in the world, anytime of the day or year. In sizes from 10 through 18 Hare's Ears seem to imitate many species of caddis flies, mayflies and even scuds. Never leave home without a good selection of these.

Wooly Worms in olive, brown and black also produce on lifts or when just cast out and allowed to slowly sink. This pattern is one of the best of all lake flies and will take trout on high mountain lakes when nothing else will even turn a fish's head out of curiosity.

And, finally, a selection of leech patterns—brown, black, purple—will save the day when fished just below the surface and not too far from shore with a slow, steady strip and then a hesitation allowing the pattern to sink a little bit. Basically, you

This is what it is all about in trout fishing. A classic riseform is made by a large cutthroat trout feeding near the surface. Determine if the fish is moving or holding in the area.

want to create an undulating motion with this fly pattern.

All of this pre-supposes that you have several dry patterns tied for local conditions—flies that you have acquired through experience or local inquiry.

Wind Is Not Always An Enemy

Casting to trout on the surface of a lake seems easier when you can see the fish working so you know they are present. When the wind is blowing, the situation changes radically from an angler's perspective, but not all that much for the trout.

Fish are more difficult to spot when the wind blows. When they are seen, they will usually be making a porpoising rise through a wave or a quick leap to snatch a bug before it is blown to oblivion. But the wind can also concentrate trout.

Surface Fishing On Lakes

Look for windrows on the surface—lanes of smooth water between the waves. Often there will be foam lines and accumulated insects and debris in these spots. Cast along the edges (seams, always seams, even on still waters) and then work gradually in through the lane of smooth water. Use the same methods as above. Trout will be present, unless you are trying to work in a raging storm, in which case you should be safely on shore talking fishing with a friend and making periodic casts out into the water to create the illusion that you are seriously fishing for trout. This is just in case anyone is watching your behavior from a concealed position.

Spinners, Then Spoons Are Good Second Choices

True, flies work best on the surface, but well-cast spinners and spoons will take plenty of trout.

Because these are heavier and make more of a splash on entry, the approach to feeding fish needs to be modified. See if you can observe a pattern to a specific trout's feeding. Is it working in a certain direction or cruising in one general area?

If the fish is heading in a certain direction, cast well ahead of it and bring the lure back through the perceived line of travel. Trout can see for long distances in lakes, so it is better to cast too far than to spook the fish by dropping the lure too close to the fish.

When the fish is working a fixed location, cast out over the area, if possible, and bring the lure back through it.

You may have to change colors or finishes (from gold to silver to copper) or even allow the lure to sink down below the trout so that it works toward the surface as you bring it back to you. This is spinning's version of the lifting technique. Count-down minnows that allow you to measure and then accurately duplicate productive depths are fantastic for this type of fishing.

For those with spinning gear who would like to use flies on lakes (or even on streams and rivers), the use of a clear plastic bubble or float will give you sufficient weight for casting a fly. Tie a blood knot about 2 feet up the line with 15 inches or more of tag end. Attach the bubble to the end of the line and the fly to the tag end. Then, fish this the same as you do dry flies. The setup does work with nymphs, but you need a much longer tag

Thermal Stratification Of A Lake

Summer Stratification
Direct—warmest water
above

Winter Stratification
Inverse—warmest water
below

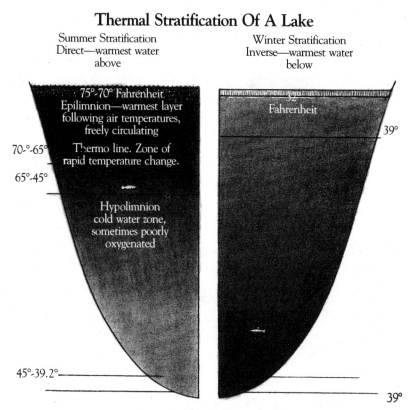

75°-70° Fahrenheit
Epilimnion—warmest layer
following air temperatures,
freely circulating

Thermo line. Zone of
rapid temperature change.

70-°-65°

65°-45°

Hypolimnion
cold water zone,
sometimes poorly
oxygenated

45°-39.2°

32
Fahrenheit

39°

39°

In the summer, warmer water tends to be at the top of a lake system and since trout prefer water below 70 degrees but above 50 degrees, that is the range an angler needs to find by probing with a thermometer in deep lakes. In the winter, the warmer water is on the bottom.

end to obtain the proper action, and this creates tangles and wind knots with frightening regularity.

Bait On Top Is Not So Hot

When trout are cruising and feeding everywhere, you would think that hooking an earthworm or hellgrammite, or anything else, on a hook with a bobber attached a couple of feet above and pitching the whole rig out onto the lake would take fish regularly.

Such is not often the case. Perhaps the shadow of the bobber or the motionless nature of the bait is too artificial or alien to the trout. For whatever reason, bait fished on the surface is a poor third to flies and spinning with one exception (always those exceptions). When there are terrestrials being

Splice Knot

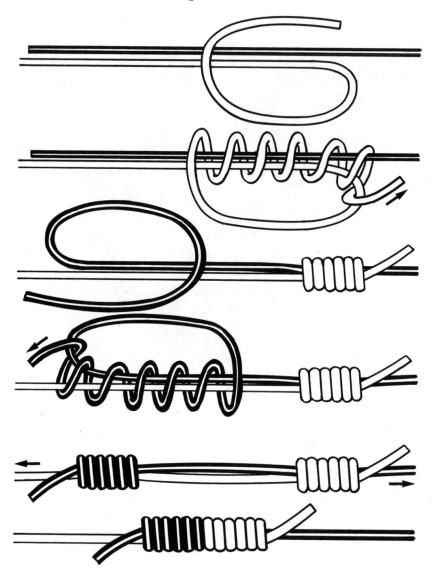

The splice knot is a handy knot to know, especially when having to make quick changes during trolling. Starting at the top, just follow the steps shown, and remember to clip the remnant ends (bottom) for a smooth, trouble-free knot.

blown out onto the water, the casting bubble setup rigged with a hopper or cricket (or whatever terrestrial insect is present) will catch fish almost as well as flies.

Side Planers And Trolling

Trolling is not by any means the best method for taking trout when they are on the surface well away from shore, such as will be discussed in Chapter 23. However, there are times when working a lure just below the surface, and as far from the boat as the side planer will allow, can catch fish.

Most of the time, if the trout are feeding on emerging aquatic insects, trolling will scare the fish off. But during times when minnows and other forage fish are being chased by big trout on the surface, trolling can be deadly.

Minnow imitations and spoons that match the size of the baitfish being chased will take plenty of trout. When there are schools of these minnows working all over the lake, the direction you troll does not seem to be critical. If a trout sees your lure, it will strike. At other times, you must try and match the direction and speed of the prey as closely as possible, which can take time.

22

Subsurface Fishing

I f the surface of a lake or reservoir can be considered a desert, the often unfathomable (no pun intended) depths of the subsurface zone is mind-boggling. While looking for trout on the surface may be difficult, finding them beneath that surface, sometimes in a hundred feet or more of water, can appear an impossible task.

But, as was seen in Chapter 10, there are natural clues, tips and keys to finding trout. With the aid of modern electronic technology, every kid on the block can own a fish locator. This device simplifies the process of searching the water of these already narrowed-down subsurface areas.

There are a variety of ways to fish this deeper water ranging from trolling to spinning to baitcasting and even using a fly rod. This latter method is more a matter of stubbornness and eccentricity, characteristics frequently associated with fly fishers, than practicality.

One thing about trolling, especially concerning lake trout, is that once you locate the fish and are able to troll a lure or bait directly through the depth at which the trout are holding, you will definitely catch them. This is not always the case with rising fish in both streams and lakes or, for that matter, most other common angling situations.

Trolling Is By Far The Best Method

If there is a more productive means of taking trout in

Working the edge of a drop-off in the evening produces big fish that come up from the depths to feed on minnows darting in the shallows.

subsurface and bottom waters than trolling, it is one well-kept secret. Even in extreme depths an angler can fish effectively with downriggers as discussed in Chapter 16. These devices are now so sophisticated and so easy to use, that NAFC members can work water depths with an accuracy bordering on a few feet or better. In big water, chasing big trout, baitcasting, or trolling reels, are preferred. Stout rods and reels with guts are needed to handle many yards of line while working in rough conditions.

When you are working big lakes for trophy fish such as lake trout, forget about other methods unless the trout have moved into the shoreline shallows (which will be dealt with in the following chapter). Trolling is the only sure-fire method for taking trout when they are down deep.

Smaller Lakes Call For A Different Approach

On smaller lakes, the depths fished can be anywhere from a couple of feet to over 40. On big waters, like the Great Lakes, the depths can be a couple of hundred feet.

On smaller waters, anglers can use spinning gear and lighter baitcasting setups. Depth is controlled by type of lure (deep-divers, shallow runners, flatfish or spinners), speed of the boat, weight attached to the line and amount of line being worked. In deep waters, downrigger weights or cannonballs, weighing 8 to 10 pounds are used to hold line to a desired depth. The advantage of the downrigger is that lighter, softer monofilament line can be used. Downriggers work best for suspended fish, or those found on deep, even bottoms, where a minimum of depth adjustment is needed over a long distance. Single-strand wire and lead-core lines are still popular for fishing deep, uneven bottom structure that can *eat* expensive cannonballs. But these heavy lines are difficult and ungainly to work with. Even so, where lake trout are found hugging rough structure, the wire or lead lines can be the most effective way to catch them.

Start Out Slowly

Unless personal experience or prevailing local wisdom dictates otherwise, the best speed at which to begin trolling is the absolute slowest you can go and still impart action to the lure. In most cases, this is *slow*—one-mile-per-hour kind of

Trout Feeding Habitats

As much as 90 percent of a trout's feeding is subsurface on minnows, scuds, nymphs, worms and even plants. Always fish weedbeds, rocky structure and around springs and other submerged objects. If no fish are found, try different depths until you find them.

slow. To give you an idea of how "fast" this is, covering the distance of a football field, end zones excluded, would take about three and one-half minutes. Many may say trolling is a "lazy" way to fish, but keeping a boat moving on a steady course and keeping track of a rod or two at this pace for any length of time takes serious concentration.

Trolling requires terminal gear that won't reduce the action of your lure. Some anglers favor attaching lures or bait hooks to the line with loops to allow the lure free movement, but ball-bearing swivels are the most durable method and they do not detract appreciably from a lure's action.

Unless you know you will be getting into very big trout, you can use line weights of 8, 6 and even 4 pounds successfully when coupled with lure weights of ⅓ ounce or less. As is the case with most fishing, try and match the gear to the size of the trout you expect to encounter. If your tackle is too light, the fish may put up a wonderful fight, but by the time it gets to the net it is as good as dead because lethal levels of lactic acid build up in the body tissues during the struggle. If you are planning on releasing the trout, forget it.

Deep Trolling Beats The Heat

Come late July and the dog days of summer, even large bodies of water such as Lake Mead in Arizona, begin to warm. Trout will not be found in the shallows, except late in the evening, if at all. Surface temperatures climb to levels uncomfortable for trout. Catching fish means going down after them wherever they may be suspended.

If depthfinders did not exist, the next best way to find trout would be to use a thermometer. As soon as you find 70-degree water, you should be closing in on fish. Find the mid-60s and you would be in prime water. Many anglers use temperature probes on smaller lakes where shallow water makes depthfinders less effective.

Cowbells Call In The Fish

One method of trolling that works extremely well, even for fish of 12 inches or less is using a string of revolving flashers, or cowbells, with a spoon, bait or possibly a streamer attached to the end. By dredging down deep and working back and forth across a lake in a systematic pattern until the fish are found, anglers using this setup can take limits of trout on the hottest and brightest of days.

Some of the more popular baits for use behind cowbells include smelt, shiners, chubs and nightcrawlers. Almost anything that leaves a scent trail for the trout to track to the lure, on the odd chance that it does not see the bright, flashing light of the spinning blades which is your basic underwater version of a Fourth of July display, will take trout. Some lead weight and a form of keel is often required to make this rig work properly at the correct depth.

This is not light-line, light-rod fishing, and unless the trout is a monster, do not expect to see it tailwalk across the lake's surface once hooked.

Hanging Out On The Bottom

There are times when trout hold just off the bottom. Trolling will take those fish, but hangups and lost gear are common when trying to work these regions. This is when bait comes into its own in deep water.

Basically simple in nature, any type of gear that lets you drop your bait down to the trout (this can be anything from earthworms to corn to baitfish to maggots) will take fish. On big lakes there is frequently enough current to drift an unweighted or lightly weighted bait well off target. Keep adding lead until the bait is holding stationary and absolutely vertical in the water.

Rarely does this fishing involve leaving the bait on the bottom, though lake trout are notorious scavengers that will pick up a dead baitfish. Rainbows are often caught by anglers who cast a salmon egg, or clump of eggs, and let the bait rest on bottom. There are two basic ways to fish bottom while drifting or trolling. One is to pay out line until the bait hits bottom and then reel in enough line so that the offering is a foot or so above bottom. The other is to leave a couple of feet (or more) of line between the bait and sinker. Then, drop the sinker to the bottom, using it as a locator to help you keep contact with the bottom as you move along. For still fishing, use egg or bank sinkers threaded to slide on the line. Fish with a free spool so that the trout can pick up the bait, run with it and pause to eat it before you set the hook.

Go On If You Must And Try Fly Fishing Gear

There are conditions where fishing deep water is practical (or at least possible) with fly fishing gear. You can troll, very slowly, with full-sinking lines and weighted streamers.

This combination will work down, but to nowhere near the depths of the other rigs. When trout are suspended maybe 10 or 20 feet below the surface, this is not as farfetched as it may first appear. Streamers have excellent action when trolled and the quicker action of most fly rods helps this along. Because fly rods are softer than baitcasting rods, setting the hook is difficult. If the trout does not hook itself on the take, your set has to be exaggerated, pulling down on the line with one hand and yanking as far back as possible with the rod hand.

Fishing a fly rod down deep on this valley lake produced good trout. Lakes formed along the sides of mountains often have deep drop-offs caused by scouring action of retreating glaciers.

Fish taken this way are fine sport due to the lightweight nature of the rod. So the advantages are good action with a streamer and good sporting qualities, but all of this applies only to moderate depths.

You can also fish bait with a fly rod in depths of up to 30 feet. Anything deeper and line control is difficult. With a sinking-tip line and a leader of 15 feet, plus a split shot or two for sinking the bait, you can work small baits like maggots and nymphs with a lifting action near the bottom. Trout really go for this and as an added bonus so do lake whitefish, which can reach up to about 10 pounds.

Casting Lures Is An Option

Any sinking lure is a candidate for working in deep water.

Heavy spoons cast far out with medium- to heavyweight gear and then allowed to sink to the bottom, can be big fish takers when they are retrieved back up through the depths. The same is true with countdown minnows, spinners and a number of other heavy lures.

In deep water, time the period the lure takes to reach bottom so that if it starts to get hung up you can shorten the depth by decreasing the length of sink time. One advantage to starting at the bottom is that you are working all levels of water on the retrieve. Fish can hit throughout the cast. You are able to cover a lot of water in a short time and do it efficiently.

Jigs Do A Number

The ever-popular leadhead jig so justifiably famous in walleye-angling circles will also take trout, though no one with a reasonable grasp on reality will ever try and suggest that this is the best way to take trout in deep water or any other water.

Casting a jig out and letting it sink to the bottom and then using a jerking, halting retrieve takes fish. Adding a piece of smelt or similar bait seems to enhance the lure.

Also, you can let the jig drop straight down to the bottom and then work it up and down in 1- or 2-foot increments in areas where you know there are trout. This action eventually takes fish for reasons only they know. Perhaps this imitates the action of a wounded baitfish or maybe the constant action eventually sets off the aggressive nature of the fish. Regardless of the reasons, there are times when jigs take trout and nothing else will. And they are not all that hard to fish in most cases.

So, when you find trout be sure and fish down to them, well below where they are suspended to be positive the offering comes through their level. On those rare occasions when trout are found but will not take, experiment. Sooner or later some combination of retrieve, lure and bait will catch fish.

=23=

Shorelines And Rivermouths

Continuing with the desert metaphor from in the previous two chapters, shorelines and rivermouths are the oases of lakes and reservoirs. They are easy-to-find areas of abundant food and feeding trout, most of the time.

Shoreline habitat can vary from rock-strewn, sandy, tree- or brush-lined, rocky drop-offs, points to small isolated back bays. Flows that enter a lake often attract trout.

Rivermouths may influence lake environments for many acres where they pour into a system, or a flow may only affect a few square feet as a tiny cold-water spring seeps into the lake. The same is true for outlets. Each of the above mentioned habitats are likely places to fish. When working unfamiliar water, keying on one of these habitats will normally turn up trout and often save NAFC members hours of futile searching on the open reaches of lakes and reservoirs.

Much of this "trouty" water is best fished from a boat, but anglers working from shore will catch their share of fish if they plan ahead and carefully work the spots available to them.

Shorelines Often Tip Their Hands

There are a number of indications of a shoreline's worth, from an angling perspective. Any one of a number of shorelines can have big fish chasing smaller fish at some time or another, but long stretches of sandy beach or yards and yards of smooth,

The inlet holds good fish all the way through the visible seams of current out in the lake. The rocky and weedy shoreline is also worth checking for cruising trout, particularly in the morning and evening.

Shorelines And Rivermouths

shallow-water rock shelf are not places to stake your fishing reputation on. There is little, if any, structure for fish to hide in. There are few rocks or boulders, little aquatic plant growth or downed trees—the kind of habitat that produces food and shelter for the fish.

Ignore these spots for the most part because they will be devoid of trout.

But, when you see a shoreline piled with boulders and larger rocks extended well out into the water, you should immediately register "trout" in your mind.

From a boat, cast into every nook and cranny, every swirling pocket of water created by wave action. Work this water thoroughly with spinners, wooden minnows and, to a lesser extent, small spoons. Streamers work well stripped through here, also. In the evenings when smaller forage fish lose some of their fear, work these lures right up to dry land. There are times when big trout can be seen feeding in water so shallow that their dorsal fins are exposed to the air.

For those casting from shore there are a couple of options. The best one is to put on hip or chest waders and work out into the lake as far as possible and fish the water as you would from a boat. One word of caution: the rocks in this type of water are often extremely slippery because they are covered with algae and moss. Wear stream cleats. They will make your efforts easier and safer.

If you prefer to "dry-land" the situation, work from rocks you can easily reach that jut out in the water. Cast into any pockets you observe and then retrieve the lure parallel to shore much as though you were trolling.

Trolling With Side Planers Covers Turf

Working this same water and all other potentially productive shorelines with side planers is an excellent way to cover a great deal of water thoroughly and without scaring off the trout.

You will want to experiment with the setup until you have the side planers working at least 25 feet from the boat and the lures just above the bottom. In the case of boulder-strewn water you may be working higher than average to avoid fouling your lure on the really big rocks. Bait like minnows works well on side planers as do spinners, flutter spoons and minnow-imitating

Uni-Knot

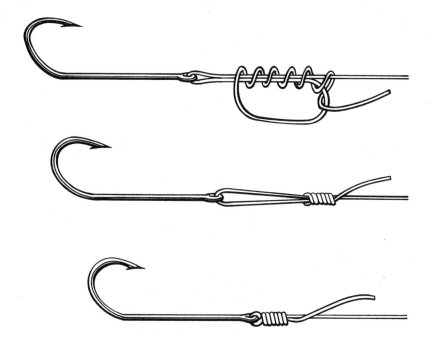

One of the best all-purpose knots, the uni-knot is tied by running at least 6 inches of line through the eye, folding it back to parallel main line (top). Bring the short end back to form a loop and make six turns with the tag end within the loop. Pull tag end to snug turns and slide resulting knot up to eye and trim tag end flush.

plugs. Because you will be working water less than 20 feet most of the time and with probably less than 100 feet of line out, medium-weight baitcasting and spinning gear is perfect for this fishing situation.

After every fish, or perhaps every 15 minutes or so, be sure and check for wear and nicks on the first few feet of your line. These can be caused by trout teeth and bouncing and rubbing along the bottom. This check only takes seconds and sure beats breaking off a nice fish due to line failure.

Gravel Is Prime During Spawning

Loose-graveled shorelines can be superb big-fish sites, especially during spawning time. All trout construct their redds, places where they deposit their eggs and milt, in gravels of varying diameters. One of the major factors in the survival of emerging fry is the amount of sediment found in spawning areas. Too much, and the eggs suffocate.

Most species of trout prefer to spawn in moving water associated with rivers and streams, but in closed systems such as reservoirs they may not be able to do this. The only major source of water in some of these areas is provided by upwelling springs and periodic discharges that are released from irrigation-channel gates.

When you know this to be the case and will be fishing during spawning time (spring for rainbows and fall for brookies), look for gravel shorelines on the windward side of the lake or reservoir. This is because you will want a location that is scoured clean by wave action that has built up as the wind whips across the water.

Trout will move up out of their deep-water holding areas and spawn in these areas. Many times the spawning is non-productive and more a matter of instinctive behavior. This does not affect the fishing. These are times when anglers can take trout of size—the biggest a system has to offer.

Casting spinners (especially those with chartreuse bodies and tails) and streamers through the spawning redds, which are discerned by their lighter color, will trigger territorial responses from the fish. Most times you will see the trout you are casting to. Early in the spawning period, many casts might be needed to trick the fish. If you time this properly, you can take fish every cast. When this is the case in waters where actual spawning replenishes a lake's population, make moderation a rule. Play these trout quickly and release them to maintain the fishery. Take pictures. *Playing* a 7-pound rainbow is ample reward for your efforts.

Fish Deep On Drop-Offs And Points
Points extending out into the water and abrupt drop-offs are places to fish bait and lures down deep. Trout hold near the bottom below this type of structure and will only come up to take a really tempting offering or during periods of very low light or darkness.

Often, these points and rock ledges are homes to thousands and thousands of nymphs—caddis, stone fly, mayfly. When this is the case, baitfishers should pluck these off the rocks for bait. When they are too small or fragile a species to work on a hook, use a maggot. This creature is an adequate substitute for larval forms that frequently have white-colored bodies.

The nymph fisher can try and coax a response with an imitation, but because of the abundance of food, chances are his pattern will go unnoticed. Fly fishers are better off using brightly colored streamers that are stripped as close to the bottom as possible.

Deep-diving minnows worked down to the bottom, then allowed to float toward the surface a few feet and retrieved again, will take trout—usually the largest of the area. Big fish get first pickings of the best food sources.

One hot spot for big fish is the downwind water extending from the tip of a point. The breeze concentrates food along this line much like a seam of current in a river. Start by casting out and working your way down and across these areas. Fly fishers using nymphs like the Prince or Sheep Creek will pick off trout casting perpendicular to the line, which will often be glassy or smooth-looking or have a foam line, letting the wind push the wider-diameter fly line "downstream." Retrieve the pattern in 18-inch to 2-foot slow, steady strips, working gradually downwind. This is world-class big-trout terrain.

Tree-lined And Brushy Banks Hide Trout

This type of cover has the same positive attributes on a lake or reservoir environment as it does on rivers and streams. Overhanging branches provide protection from avian predation. Also, countless insects hatch and fall from these branches into the water below.

Trout will frequently feed in only inches of water and casting into shore from a float tube or canoe can create excellent sport for the fly fisher matching what is seen on the water's surface. Minnows and bait are less productive because fish are extremely wary in the shallows and they are also fixated on aquatic insects.

When there are downed logs or limbs extending out into deep water, though, minnow imitations, small spoons and spinners cast along the length of the object will bring up fish. If the log is under the water, work the lure below the bottom edge. This is where the trout will be holding. A higher retrieve will probably not be seen by the fish.

Any sheltered bank or downed log or pile of logs, not to mention abandoned beaver lodges along the shore, is worthy of at least a few minutes of an angler's time. Forget working around active beaver lodges. Trout are not suicidal by nature.

Bays Offer Protection

Wherever there are well-defined bays, tight loops away from the main body of water or fertile crescents protected from the weather by the shoreline, you will find trout.

Trolling the edges of these areas either directly behind the boat or off to the side with minnows for bait or with spoons or minnow imitations is a sound practice. You will need to work as

Anglers can take nice trout from shore as this photo demonstrates. Looking for feeding fish or casting to weedbeds and submerged structures is a good way to approach this situation.

Stream inlets such as this one are good spots to prospect for trout. Drift the offering downstream into the lake. The rocky shoreline to the left will also hold trout that forage among the boulders for minnows and aquatic insects.

close to the bottom as possible where the trout are holding, protected from predation in the lesser light.

Wading out or casting from shore to weedbeds also works. Working a nymph or spinner just above the tops of this kind of aquatic growth will bring trout out of hiding. They feel safe rushing up to grab food and then being able to charge back down the few inches to cover. Work between any reeds and weedbeds, too.

As with any trout water, still or moving, always fish obstructions extending out into a bay or fixed in the water. These spots hide fish and provide habitat for their food sources. Rocky bays like those associated with the northern shores of the Great Lakes are good examples of this type of water, especially around river mouths.

Shorelines And Rivermouths

Working The Concentrated Food Sources

Lake inlets (A) and outlets (B) provide food, shelter and increased oxygen levels in abundance as do springs (C). Brush piles, deadfalls (D), reefs, drop-offs (E) and islands (F) provide shelter and food but moving or bubbling flows are required to oxygenate water. Moss or weedbeds (G) always hold good numbers of aquatic insects, scuds and minnows. Long points (H) create eddies that concentrate food sources.

Inlets And Outlets Are Logical Choices

Trout will always be found around inlets and outlets. Cast right up into them and work your lure or fly first down along the seams between the swirling water and the calm of the lake and then gradually inward through the tongue of the main current. Start at the bottom and work up, giving each depth and line of retrieve several casts before moving over.

Outlets are choice locations for forage fish, so spinfishers should concentrate on sinking or diving minnow imitations and heavy spoons that will sink down to the bottom. Spoons with bright-metal finishes are best since they reflect what light is available, attracting the trout.

Baitfishers using minnows should add enough weight to hold the rig in one spot on the bottom, leaving enough line between the sinker and hook to allow the bait to swing naturally in the current. Worms are not a bad idea in these places, either.

Trolling down deep, around the entrances of big rivers requires plenty of weight, but may be the only consistent method for taking the trout that are holding many feet below the surface. Strong currents associated with large rivers are moderated along the streambottom, giving the fish a chance to rest and feed. Fish will rarely be found much above this region in the harsher flows.

For the fly fisher, streamers worked down deep will catch trout, but this may not be possible to do in heftier flows. In that case, attention should be directed to side eddies and smaller chutes found near shore away from the main current stem. Weighted nymphs worked along the bottom also work well. Sinking lines and short leaders of 3 or 4 feet should be used. They provide better line control, and an angler can detect a strike quicker.

Outlets can often include deep pools formed behind obstructions. During the day, trout may be down deep and methods used for deep pools work well. Fish can also be resting under accumulations of logs, foam or other debris, so working right along the edges or, in the case of foam, right in the middle, takes fish.

One place you will not find trout is in the shallow-water runs connecting lakes with rivers. The fish may be stacked up in the deep water just before the stream, or in a river's pools, but the only time trout will be in this shallow, moving water is when they are transferring from one environment to another. They are on the run, intent upon getting through the danger zone as quickly as possible. Concentrate your attentions above and below the runs, fishing down deep or casting to any downed logs or rock outcroppings—any shelter immediately to the sides of the outlet. Trout will go for the first available cover.

=24=

Ice Fishing For Trout

Those who do not ice fish and might happen to drive by a cluster of anglers perched on a frozen lake or reservoir have a common misconception concerning ice fishing. Seeing a dozen or more people fishing in a relatively confined area, the uninitiated assume that the lake (in one spot at least) is heavily fished.

Actually, nothing could be further from the truth when comparing the same water in warm weather, a time when numerous boats are either anchored or trolling the same area over and over and still other anglers are flinging lures, flies and bait to the same location from shoreline positions.

Trout Are Not Pressured In Winter

Trout are really not pressured in the winter. Ice fishing offers a chance to escape the confines of home in the dead of winter, get some fresh (though brisk in nature) air and maybe even a touch of sunshine, all while catching a dinner or two's worth of trout.

And, if you like your isolation, you can always ski, snowmobile or snowshoe into your favorite lake and fish among the awesome stillness and soft beauty of winter.

Plus, consider a major advantage in your favor. NAFC members can stand right on top of the fish they are after with absolutely no fear of discovery by the trout who are suspended in the chill darkness below, oblivious to the activity raging

The dedicated ice fisherman searching for trout stays completely portable without a portable ice fishing house to worry about. Note that he does use a depthfinder to help him locate fish.

Ice Fishing For Trout

above them. Actually, in the ice-on period, the water most fish will be caught in is warmer than the air you will be standing in. The liquid will certainly be above freezing, for obvious reasons.

Another misconception concerning ice fishing is that all a person has to do is drill a hole in the ice, jam a piece of bait on a hook with a few sinkers twirling above it and plunk the mess through the hole to catch fish. There is a little more to the practice than this, and there are a number of tricks that will simplify and improve your catch rate.

First, and foremost, dress warmly, but in layers that can be easily shed or put back on as the weather changes. You can easily be warm enough to fish in shirt sleeves in mid-January when the sun comes out and reflects off the snow and ice. Rubber pac-type insulated boots are a good idea. Cold, wet feet will spoil a day's fishing. Bring along a bucket to sit on and haul home your trout in, a dipper to keep the hole free of ice. An ice auger to drill the hole and a sled or daypack to carry gear are needed. A gas stove is a wonderful addition, allowing you to brew warm liquids and have a hot meal out on the ice. No one said ice fishing could not be a great time, now, did they? Sunglasses for bright days are a necessity. Snow blindness hurts—a lot.

Jigging Is A Popular Method

Perhaps the most popular method for catching trout through the ice is by the easily learned jigging method. Tackle, as with most ice fishing gear, is straightforward and inexpensive. Short rods and the most basic of reels are needed. In fact, one of the most efficient rods can be easily made by taking that 2-foot or so tip section of your favorite spinning rod that broke in the car door last summer and gluing a cork handle on the butt end. The flex, strength and feel of graphite rods are ideal qualities in an ice fishing setup.

Special cold water monofilament lines are available now that retain their supple, responsive characteristics in very frigid conditions. The rest of the fishing tackle is basic in nature and will be detailed shortly.

Jigging through the ice is usually used when smaller trout—12 to 15 inches—in large numbers are anticipated. The rest of the equipment consists of 6-pound test line, a reel that

Snowmobiles provide winter access to hard-to-reach lakes. These fishermen have towed their gear with them for quick set up.

allows you to keep track of depth through counting the number of turns needed to reach the level where the trout are, No. 12 to No. 14 hooks, split shot for weight, snap swivels for ease in changing hooks and a good supply of maggots. These should be kept as warm as possible stored inside your coat so they won't freeze and lose their freshness.

Experienced ice fishers have their favorite baits ranging from worms to corn to marshmallows, but the lowly maggot takes trout with a consistency that is hard to beat. An exception is with tip-up rigs when minnows are used to attract larger trout. This will be discussed shortly.

When you find the fish beneath the ice, they will often be in schools, so if they are deep you need to know exactly how many turns of line are required to reach the productive level.

Ice Fishing For Trout

Jigging for trout requires constant attention. This fisherman is using the jig-and-snatch technique because most trout taken in deep water are taken without fishermen feeling a bite.

Schools frequently move from spot to spot so it is important to maximize your time in the water.

When jigging in deep water, most trout are taken without feeling the bite. Instead the jig-and-snatch technique is used, alternately lifting the bait slightly and then jerking upward. The theory is that a trout will take on the soft lift, and the hook is then set on the snatch. The proper jigging interval becomes intuitive with experimentation and experience.

Tip-Up Fishing For Larger Fish

The purpose of a tip-up rig is not to take large numbers of small trout but to catch big fish. They are ideal for lake trout. An effective and serious tip-up angler uses as many rigs as is legally allowed at his favorite spots.

While on this subject, the best places to fish for trout in winter are often the best spots to work in summer, provided they have sufficient depth for the trout to suspend, and that the lake is deep enough to contain adequate oxygen to carry the fish through a long, ice-darkened winter. Of course, portable depthfinders can help you locate fish, but another good and simple method of choosing an ice-fishing location is to drill a hole in an area containing numerous frozen-over holes from previous angling efforts. If you see signs of fish having been cleaned or perhaps that of an old fire, you know that you are closing in on trout.

Tip-ups are designed to hold a baited line, plus reserve line and to alert the angler to a bait immediately, usually by a red flag springing up when a trout tugs at line on the tilt.

When using minnows, attaching them to Russian spoons or Swedish Pimples add to the trout-taking ability of the setup. The little bit of flash draws in trout. Small ice-jigs also have the potential of catching trout.

Spring bobbers are devices that detect even the smallest of takes. They are simply a thick wire or thin flat piece of metal that is an extension of your rod and will indicate the slightest change down below. The big advantage is that when a trout is holding the bait but no movement has been shown, raising the rod slightly will make the bobber drop, saying "fish on." Many takes in the winter are extremely subtle and this system is a big help under these conditions.

Ice Fishing Cures Mid-Winter Blues

If you are not a dyed-in-the-wool ice fisher, you probably wonder why anyone would go outdoors in the dead of winter to be beat up by rough weather. There is something magical about taking trout through the ice. The sport is a refinement and an extension of the excitement anglers have experienced the first time a fish pulled their bobber underwater.

Ice fishing can produce fast-paced fishing and at midday with the sun beating down overhead, the temperature can be "balmy." On many days with bright-light conditions during the summer, there is no way you could catch trout. Not so in the winter. The ice blocks out most of the light and the trout don't know the difference. Not a bad way to spend a day.

Index